MW00388600

PACEMAKER®

# Practical English

PACEMAKER®

# Practical English

GLOBE FEARON
Pearson Learning Group

**Pacemaker® Practical English Third Edition**

**REVIEWERS**
We thank the following educators, who provided valuable comments and suggestions during the development of this book:

***Pacemaker Curriculum Advisor:*** Stephen Larsen, formerly of the University of Texas at Austin

***Subject Area Consultants:*** M.B. Clarke, University of California, Davis, and A.G. Clarke, American River College, Sacramento

*Executive Editor:* Eleanor Ripp
*Project Editor:* Brian Hawkes
*Assistant Editor:* Alisa Brightman
*Lead Designer:* Tricia Battipede
*Research Manager:* Angela Darchi
*Marketing Manager:* Katie Erezuma
*Production Editor:* Angela Dion
*Manufacturing Supervisor:* Mark Cirillo
*Cover Design:* Tricia Battipede

**About the Cover:** English skills help people communicate effectively with one another. The images on the cover show the variety of ways that English skills are used in everyday life. Computers are used to give and receive information. "Help Wanted" ads show listings of available jobs. Daily planners help people organize themselves. Letters and postcards are mailed to keep in touch with loved ones. Job applications need to be filled in to get jobs. What are some other ways you use English skills in your life?



ISBN 0-130-23606-3

Printed in the United States of America
5 6 7 8 06 05 04 03

**1-800-321-3106**
**www.pearsonlearning.com**

# Contents

## A Note to the Student

The purpose of this book is to help you develop the English skills you need to succeed in today's world. You will learn how good English skills can help you in all areas of your life. A solid understanding of the English skills in this book will help you not only at school, but at home, on the job, in your community, and even in your free time.

For example, one of the units in this book covers the English skills you will need to look for a job and to interview for a job. This unit also covers some of the skills you will need once you get the job.

Throughout the book, you will have plenty of opportunities to practice the skills you are learning. The "Chapter Projects" and "Group Activities" give you the opportunity to practice skills with your classmates. Practicing these skills will help you now and for the rest of your life. Remember that practice makes perfect.

You will also find notes in the margins of the pages. The "Brush Up on the Basics" margin notes remind you of grammar rules that apply to the skill you are learning. The "English and Careers" margin notes show you how the skills you are learning will apply when you are at work. The "English and Technology" margin notes explain how technology such as computers can help you master the skills you are learning. The "Everyday English" margin notes connect the skills to your everyday life. Finally, the "English Tip" margin notes highlight important concepts and tips related to the skills you are learning.

In addition, you will find several study aids in the book. At the beginning of every chapter you will find "Learning Objectives." They will help you focus on the important points in the chapter. You will also find "Words to Know," a look ahead at new vocabulary words you will find in the chapter. The colorful photos, charts, and drawings in the book will bring the English skills to life. Finally, you will find a "Chapter Summary" at the end of each chapter before the "Chapter Review." Use the summaries to make sure you understand the skills you have just learned.

Everyone who put this book together worked hard to make it useful, interesting, and enjoyable. The rest is up to you. We wish you well in your studies. Our greatest success is in your accomplishment.

# Unit 1 English for Learning

## Chapter 1
## Everyday Living

## Chapter 2
## Using Books

## Chapter 3
## Using a Library

## Chapter 4
## Passing Tests

*Understanding and following directions is an important skill, not just on the field but in everyday life.*

# Chapter 1 Everyday Living

## Words to Know

| | |
|---|---|
| **key words** | the most important written or spoken words in a sentence, paragraph, or text |
| **main idea** | the central thought or key piece of information that is written or spoken |
| **organize** | to put things into clear order |

### Interview Project

Work with a partner and interview each other. Find out about your partner's favorite sport or musical instrument and how it is played. Take notes as you listen. Switch roles. Then organize your notes to write directions about how to play your partner's favorite sport or musical instrument.

### Learning Objectives

- Identify three ways that study skills can be useful in everyday life.
- Take complete notes on who, what, why, where, when, and how something happened.
- Organize and interpret directions.
- Identify three techniques for reviewing and remembering information in notes.

## HOW ENGLISH SKILLS CAN HELP

To get along in this world, you need to learn and remember new information, such as how to operate a VCR or DVD, or how to read a bus schedule. Other everyday learning takes place in school.

Learning and remembering information is also important to your future. Today, bank computers give out money, and telephone answering machines and voice mail take your messages. Who will get the best jobs? People who are best at adjusting to the changes in a fast-changing world.

Learning and practicing English skills can help you. Here are two of the most important skills.

- Taking notes
- Following directions

## Practice

Use a separate sheet of paper to answer these questions.

**1.** What are three everyday situations in which you read or listen to new information?

**2.** How can remembering information help you reach your goals? Write a paragraph giving examples.

**3.** Why is it a good idea to have a study partner while you are learning to take notes?

**Brush Up on the Basics**

A paragraph has a topic sentence, at least three supporting sentences, and a concluding sentence. (See Grammar 1 in the Reference Guide.)

## SKILL 1.1 Taking Notes

Taking notes is a helpful skill. The most common place you take notes is in the classroom. A history teacher may talk to you for 30 minutes about World War II, or you may take a computer class. In either case, you write down the most important information in your notes and study it later.

You can also take notes outside the classroom. Suppose you are watching a cooking show on TV. You could take notes to remember a step-by-step recipe or how to get to a new friend's house. There are a million and one uses for notes.

### How to Take Notes

You can take notes whether you are reading or listening. Taking notes involves writing down the fewest **key words**, or most important words, to get the most meaning. What key words should you look or listen for? Usually these words answer one or more of these questions:

- who?
- what?
- why?
- where?
- when?
- how?

**English Tip**
Before taking notes on anything, ask yourself this question: *What bits of information are most important to remember?*

Answering these questions will help you remember the **main idea**, or central thought, of what you have heard or read. These questions will also help you remember important details and facts.

Here are two examples of information that you might hear or read. Following each example are notes. Read through them.

**Example 1:**

A history lesson from a book

During World War II, the United States and its allies had to send secret messages back and forth. They wanted a code that the enemy could not read but that could be quickly decoded. They used many different codes. Some of them were mathematical codes. Some of them used nonsense words. One code even used a Native American language. Anyone who did not know the language found the message impossible to understand.

*Notes*

*WW II: U.S. and allies need codes. Some codes: math, nonsense, Native American language.*

**Example 2:**

Spoken directions to a friend's house

Do you remember Anthony Jones? You know, the guy who always wears those weird hats. Remember, he's got a dog? Well, the meeting is at his house today at 1:30. Just go from your house to Main Street. Hey, did you know they are tearing down the old school on Main? Anyway, go north on Main to Oak, and turn right.

Go about four blocks, or maybe it's five. I can never remember. I have such a bad memory. His house is at 401 Oak. It's on the right. There's a big old green car sitting in the front. He's had that thing for a year and it still doesn't run.

Notes

*Meeting at Anthony's. 1:30 today. North on Main. Right on Oak. 401 on right. Green car in front.*

**English Tip**
Write your notes in any form that works for you. Shorten or abbreviate words. Use short or long sentences, or don't use sentences at all. Just be sure to include the key words and the main idea.

## Practice

Use a separate sheet of paper to answer these questions.

1. For each of the examples above, what are the *who, what, why, where, when,* and *how* questions that were answered in the notes?

2. Did you get the main idea from the notes? If not, how would you change the notes?

### After You Take Notes

Notes are helpful only if you use them. If you are taking notes in class, review them the same day. Read them aloud to keep the information fresh. Talk them over with a study partner, or rewrite the information in a short paragraph. You may find something missing, or you may think of questions that you want to have answered. For instance, in Example 1 on page 6, you might ask: *What Native American Language was it? Is the code still used today?* Asking such questions helps you remember old information and learn new things along the way.

### Tips for Taking Notes

Here are the most important things to remember about taking notes.

1. Always keep paper and a pen or pencil handy.
2. Before you take notes, think about what you want to learn and how you will use the information.
3. Listen or read for key words. These words should answer the questions *who, what, why, where, when,* and *how.* They should also give you the main idea of what you are reading.
4. Notes should be short. They should have the fewest possible words and a lot of meaning.
5. Do not worry about writing complete sentences or using punctuation correctly.
6. Review your notes as needed—once a day for school notes is a good idea.

**Everyday English**

Look back at Example 2 on page 6. Is there something else you might ask your friend to help you find Anthony's house? When would be the best time to review your notes?

## Practice

Listen to the evening news for at least ten minutes. Take notes on three news stories. Follow the *Tips for Taking Notes* listed above. Bring your notes with you to class tomorrow. Be prepared to use your notes to report on what you have learned.

## SKILL 1.2 Following Directions

- You get ink on your new shirt. How do you get it clean?
- You have a homework assignment. How do you get started?
- You buy a package of noodles. How long do you cook them?

Luckily, many of these everyday problems can be solved by following directions. Directions are everywhere. They are on the tags of your clothes and in your car manual. Directions, sometimes in the form of pictures, can be found on your telephone, TV, and VCR. Many of these directions are so easy to follow that you hardly ever think about them.

*Some signs give information without words.*

**Everyday English**

Signs often give important information. What does this sign tell you?

What happens when directions are poorly written or hard to follow? Your first step is to **organize** the information, or put things into clear order.

### Organizing Information

Good step-by-step directions are written in the order in which they should be carried out. Recipes are often written this way. Here is an example.

1. Place about 1 inch of water in a pot and bring to a boil.
2. Add 4 cups of turnip greens.
3. Cover pot, and reduce flame to medium-low.
4. Simmer for 2–3 minutes, until greens are tender but still bright green.
5. Remove, drain, and place in a serving bowl.

These directions are clear and easy to follow.

What if your teacher gives you these directions in class?

> OK, I want everybody to finish this homework by Friday. I want a book report on *The Outsiders.* Turn in an outline by Wednesday because I want to make sure you're on the right track. Don't try to write the report without reading the book. Make the report three pages long and use your English book for help. Read Chapter 7 in your English book before you get started. It's on writing outlines and reports.

To turn these into useful directions, you need to figure out the correct order of the steps. Here is how they might look in the right order.

1. Read Chapter 7 in my English book.
2. Read *The Outsiders*.
3. Make an outline for my book report Tuesday and turn it in Wednesday.

**English and Technology**

You can use the *Cut* and *Paste* features of a word processing program to help you organize your notes. Then you can save or print a copy to use later.

4. Get teacher's OK to do report.
5. Do a three-page report by Thursday.
6. Turn in my report on Friday.

The directions are now step by step in the order in which they should be done. They are written in simple form. Sometimes, people in a hurry do not want to take the time to organize directions. However, organizing can save you time and energy in the long run.

### Reading Directions Carefully

Once you have organized directions, you need to read them carefully. This means reading each sentence slowly and out loud, if necessary. Read sentences over and over again until you are sure you understand their meaning. Otherwise, you might make costly mistakes. What would happen if you baked a cake at 550° instead of 350°? What would happen if you connected the jumper cables on a car the wrong way? Problems like these can be avoided if you read directions thoroughly and carefully.

## Practice

Think of one situation in which misreading directions could be harmful. Write it down on a separate sheet of paper. Then explain how you can keep such a disaster from happening to you.

## Tips for Following Directions

Here are some more helpful tips for following directions.

**Everyday English**

What is something you learned how to do by following written or spoken directions?

1. When you are listening to directions, take notes. Organize the information later if you need to.

2. Read written directions all the way through before you do anything. Then you will know whether the information needs to be reorganized. A careful reading will tell you what you need and what is expected of you.

3. Have all the needed materials on hand before you carry out any steps. This will keep you focused and organized.

4. Read each step at least twice before you carry it out. Reading out loud sometimes gives you a clearer understanding.

5. Double-check what you have done after each step.

6. If you need help, ask for it. Product manuals often list a phone number. Call this toll free number if you do not understand something. Sometimes a friend or relative can help, too.

## Practice

Read the following directions. On a separate sheet of paper, rewrite them in the order in which they should be done. Then do the steps.

Write your name (last name first) in the top right corner of a sheet of paper. Write your teacher's name in the top left corner and the name of your school above that. Write down three things you learned to do by reading directions. Before you do any of this, make sure you look over the *Tips for Following Directions* on page 12.

Chapter

# 1 Review

## Summary

Every day, for school, home, work, and play, you need to learn and remember information. Taking notes and following instructions are two skills that can make learning and remembering easier.

Taking notes is a way to break down a lot of information into small pieces. Notes usually contain key words that help you answer the questions *who, what, why, where, when,* and *how.* They help you remember the main idea of what a person said or wrote.

Study notes for school are most useful if you review them every day.

Other notes, such as directions to a friend's house, should be reviewed just before you need to perform the task.

Following directions is an important skill. Good directions are usually given in step-by-step form. Sometimes you have to rewrite directions to get them in order. It is a good idea to read directions carefully before carrying them out.

| key words |
|---|
| main idea |
| organize |

## Vocabulary Review

**Complete each sentence with a term from the box. Use a separate sheet of paper.**

1. The central thought in information that is written or spoken is called the ____.
2. The most important words in written or spoken information are called the ____.
3. To put things into an order that is easily understood is to ____.

## Chapter Quiz

**Answer the following questions in one or two sentences. Use a separate sheet of paper.**

1. Why are note taking and following directions called "everyday skills"?
2. What questions do good notes answer?
3. How detailed should notes be? Explain.
4. Should anyone be able to read your notes? Explain.
5. How can you make the best use of school notes?
6. What are two tips for taking good notes?
7. What are two everyday situations in which you might need to follow directions?
8. Why might you need to rewrite directions?
9. Why is it important to read directions carefully?

## Critical Thinking

Can note taking and following directions work together? Think of at least one situation where they do. Write it down on a separate sheet of paper.

### Group Activity

Work with a small group to write a script about someone who learns how to follow directions the hard way. Include one scene that shows the person having difficulty figuring something out, a second scene in which the person realizes he or she needs to read the directions, and a third scene with the outcome of the decision to read directions. Use a chart to help plan your script. Perform your script for the class.

Many books have a table of contents, a glossary, and an index. Knowing how to use the parts of a book makes finding information easier.

# Chapter 2 Using Books

## Words to Know

| | |
|---|---|
| **table of contents** | a list of chapters or articles found at the front of a book or magazine |
| **index** | a list of subjects and their page numbers found at the back of a book |
| **appendix** | additional information found at the back of a book |
| **glossary** | a list of definitions of special words in a section found at the back of a book |
| **scan** | to look quickly through written material |
| **trend** | a general movement in a certain direction |
| **illustration** | a drawing or photograph |
| **caption** | words that tell about an illustration |

## Idea Web Project

Make an idea web listing the ways you can find information in a book. Write the words *Ways to Find Information in a Book* in the middle circle. In each of the outer circles, write one way to find information in a book. As you read the chapter, compare your ideas with the ones listed in the book. Edit your idea web by adding new ways to find information from a book.

## Learning Objectives

- Find information using the table of contents, index, appendix, and glossary.
- Scan headings for areas of interest.
- Interpret charts and graphs.
- Use illustrations to find information.

## SKILL 2.1 Interpret a Table of Contents

At the front of most books and magazines is a **table of contents.** A table of contents lists all the titles of chapters or articles and the pages on which they begin. Sometimes a table of contents gives a description of what is in each chapter or article. Look at this example of a table of contents.

### How to Buy a Good Used Car

TABLE OF CONTENTS



### Practice

Use the table of contents above to answer the following questions. Write in complete sentences on a separate sheet of paper.

1. You are worried about getting cheated. You want to know what rights you have if you buy a bad used car. Which chapter should you read? What page number does it start on?

**Brush Up on the Basics**

A sentence has a subject and a predicate. A complete sentence makes sense on its own. (See Grammar 1–9 in the Reference Guide.)

2. You are interested in a 1996 model. Which chapter will tell you what you want to know? What page number does it start on?

3. What information might you find in Chapter 1?

## SKILL 2.2 Interpret an Index

You want to look up a very specific piece of information about a car. You do not have to read an entire chapter.

You can use an **index** to help you find what you want to know. An index is a list found in the back of many books. It lists the key subjects of the book in alphabetical order. It also gives the page numbers on which the subject can be found. Below is part of the index of *How to Buy a Good Used Car.*

**Everyday English**

Think about the ways an index helps the reader. When do you use this reader aid?

**Index**

### Take a Closer Look

Notice that some of the subjects are broken down into subheadings. For example, you can find general information under the heading **Batteries.** The two subheadings under batteries tell you where to find specific information. For example, "used batteries" are discussed on page 27.

Indexes do not list every subject in the book. Sometimes the subjects you are looking for are not easy to find. Before using an index, think of several ways a subject could be listed. For example, suppose you want to read about the dangers of leaking battery acid. You could look under **Acid, Battery,** or **Repair.** You would probably find the information you need under one of those headings.

## Practice

Use a separate sheet of paper to answer these questions.

**1.** Use the index of this book. On what page number(s) will you find information on libraries?

**2.** You want to look up the repair record of a 1997 Graceland Classic car. What are three subject headings you could look under?

## SKILL 2.3 Use an Appendix and a Glossary

You are reading through a book. You come across the words: *See Appendix.* An **appendix** is a section found at the back of a book. It includes extra, helpful information. Sometimes maps, charts, and illustrations are in the appendix.

A **glossary** is another helpful section at the back of some books. A glossary is like a dictionary. It lists key words found in the book. It also lists their meanings.

**Everyday English**

When is it better to use a glossary rather than a dictionary?

### Practice

Use a separate sheet of paper to answer these questions.

1. Look at the back of this book. Is there an appendix?
2. Look up the term *card catalog* in the glossary of this book. What does it mean?
3. What kind of information might be found in the appendix of *How to Buy a Good Used Car?* Write at least one idea.

## SKILL 2.4 Use Headings

**Everyday English**

Look in two other books. See how many "built-in features" you can find.

Most books have built-in signposts, or clues, called subtitles, or headings. The phrase ***Skill 2.4 Use Headings*** just above this paragraph is a heading. Well-written headings tell you what you are about to read. When you are looking for specific information, **scan,** or quickly look through, the headings in a chapter. Skip the headings that do not look useful to you.

Try it yourself. Which heading in this chapter would you look under if you wanted to read about glossaries?

## SKILL 2.5 Read Charts and Graphs

You finally find what you are looking for in the used car book. The information you need is neatly put together in a chart. A chart is a listing of facts in table form. Reading charts is an important language skill. Information is presented in rows (going across) and columns (going up and down). The shaded arrows in the example below show how you can use the rows and columns to find information you want.

**Average Number of Repairs Needed in First Year**

| | 1996 | 1997 | 1998 |
|---|---|---|---|
| Classic | 3 | 3 | 5 |
| Gopher | 1 | 1 | 0 |
| Rough Rider | 0 | 0 | 2 |

- The chart title tells you that you can find each car's first-year repair record.
- The columns tell you the year the car was made.
- The rows tell you the model of the car.

To find the repair record of a 1998 Gopher, follow these steps:

1. Find the column labeled 1998.
2. Find the row labeled "Gopher."
3. Run one finger down the column and one finger across the row until they meet.
4. The box tells you the 1998 Gopher needed no repairs in its first year.

## Practice

Use the chart to answer these questions. Write your answers on a separate sheet of paper.

**1.** How many times was the 1997 Classic in the shop?

**2.** Which car listed had the worst repair record?

**3.** Which was the best year for the Gopher?

### Using Pie Charts

A pie chart is a special kind of chart. Its slices stand for different numbers. A pie chart is often used to show how something is divided. The sizes of the pie pieces tell you how the different numbers compare to one another.

This pie chart shows one person's monthly budget. How much is in this person's budget for car repairs?

**Everyday English**

Make your own pie chart of a school day. Divide the pie into two pieces: the time you spend in class and the hours you have of free time.

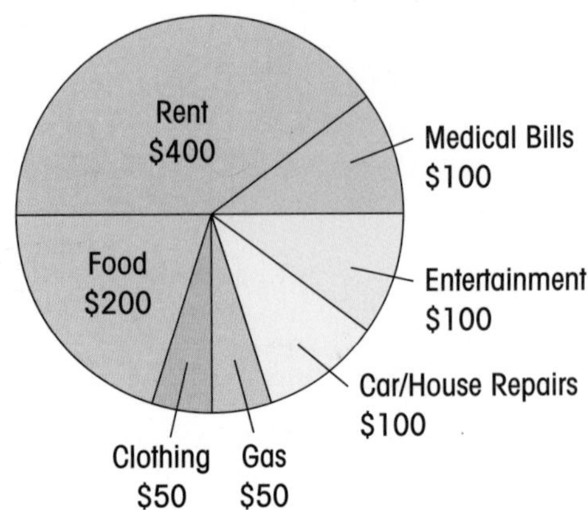


## Using Line Graphs

You have just bought a 1999 Rough Rider and you have decided to take a road trip. You want to visit your cousin in Detroit, Michigan, in July. You need to figure out what kind of clothing you should take.

You go to a library and check out the *Michigan Travel Guide.* In the index, you look up "Detroit" and "temperatures." You turn to the page listed and find a line graph showing average monthly temperatures. Take a look at the line graph below.

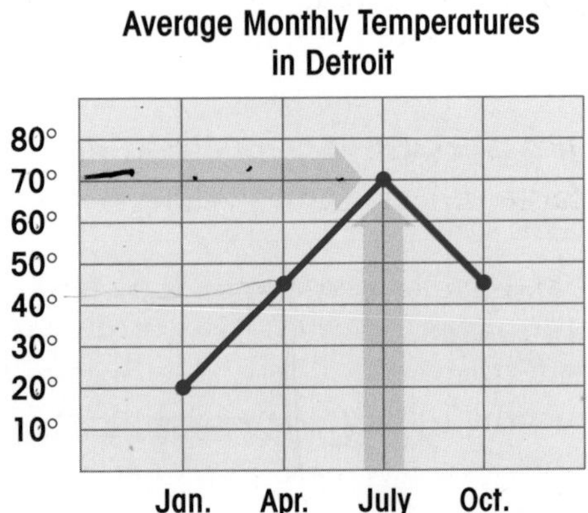

The shaded arrows show how you might find the average monthly temperature in July. Try it yourself, using the steps below.

1. Put one finger on July.
2. Run your finger up the graph until it hits the point above July.
3. Now run your finger across the graph until you hit the temperatures.
4. You can see that in Detroit it is around 70 degrees in July.

Line graphs also show **trends.** A trend is the general direction in which something is moving. The trend from January to July in Detroit is for temperatures to get warmer.

## Practice

Use the line graph to answer the following questions. Write your answers on a separate sheet of paper.

**1.** What is Detroit's average monthly temperature in April?

**2.** What kind of clothing would you need to be comfortable in Detroit in January? Why?

**3.** What is Detroit's temperature trend from July to October?

### Using Bar Graphs

Books and magazines sometimes contain bar graphs. A bar graph uses bars or boxes to present information. Bar graphs can show trends and compare information.

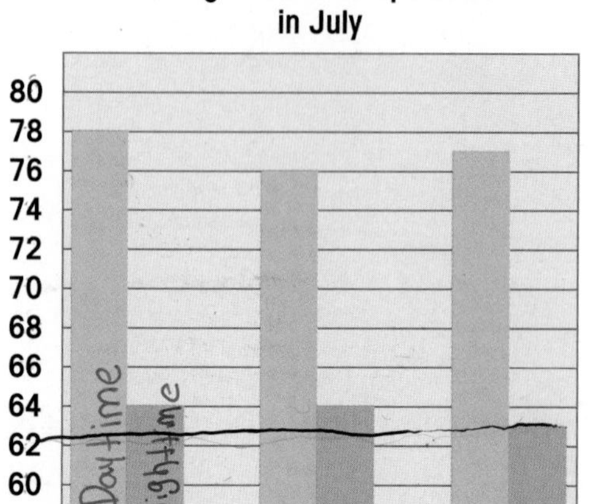


The bar graph above compares the high and low Detroit temperatures for three days in July. The tan bars show daytime high temperatures. The blue bars show nighttime low temperatures.

1. Put your finger on the blue bar above July 4th.
2. Run your finger to the top of the bar.
3. Run your finger directly across to the temperatures.
4. Your finger should show the temperature to be around 64 degrees.

You can also compare the daytime and nighttime temperatures for trends. Would you say it is warmer at night or in the daytime?

## Practice

Use a separate sheet of paper to answer these questions.

1. What was the daytime temperature in Detroit on July 4th?
2. What was the nighttime temperature on July 6th?
3. What might you pack to prepare for the difference in daytime and nighttime temperatures?

## SKILL 2.6 Use Illustrations

You can get information by looking at **illustrations**, or drawings. **Captions**, or words that tell about an illustration, often add meaning to what you see. What do you learn from this illustration and its caption?

*Most auto mechanics learn their trade on the job. Many also join apprenticeship programs. They get classroom training there as well.*

Chapter

# 2 Review

## Summary

| Books and magazines have built-in features. They are the table of contents, the index, the appendix, the glossary, and headings. These features are there to help you find information quickly and easily. |
|---|
| Charts present information in table form. A pie chart is a special kind of chart that divides information into pieces. |
| Line graphs and bar graphs also present information. They are used for showing trends and comparing information. |
| Illustrations and their captions provide important information. |

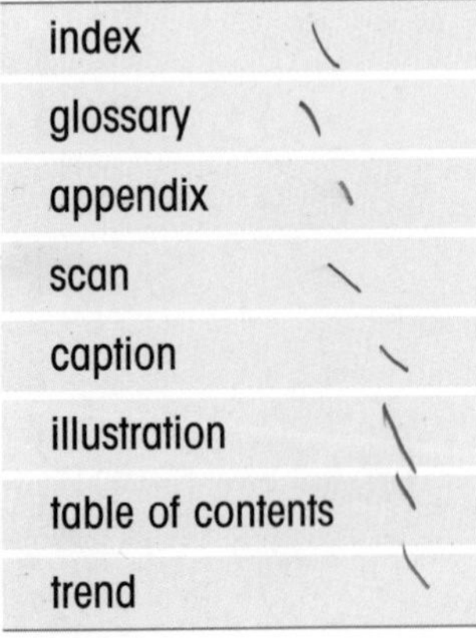

| |
|---|
| index |
| glossary |
| appendix |
| scan |
| caption |
| illustration |
| table of contents |
| trend |

## Vocabulary Review

**Match each term in the box with its meaning. Write the term and its matching number on a separate sheet of paper.**

1. a list of words and their definitions
2. words that tell about an illustration
3. to look quickly through written material
4. a list of subjects and the page numbers on which they can be found
5. additional information in the back of a book
6. a general movement in a certain direction
7. a drawing or photograph
8. a list of chapters or articles at the front of a book or magazine

## Chapter Quiz

**Answer the following questions in one or two sentences. Use a separate sheet of paper.**

1. What are four built-in features of most books?
2. How are these built-in features useful?
3. How are the index and the glossary similar to and different from each other?
4. What is a pie chart?
5. What do the slices in a pie chart stand for?
6. When would you scan headings in a book?
7. What is a trend?
8. How is a bar graph different from a line graph?
9. How can illustrations be useful?
10. How are charts and graphs useful?

## Critical Thinking

Which feature of a book or magazine could help you take notes? Give an example. Write your answer on a separate sheet of paper.

## Group Activity

Work with a small group to discuss what would be different if books no longer had the built-in features you read about in this chapter. One group member takes notes during the discussion. The remaining group members write a short essay about how much harder it would be to find information in books. In the essay, discuss the table of contents, the index, the glossary, and headings.

A computerized card catalog at a library lets you search for books, magazines, CD-ROMs, and other library sources by title, author, subject, and key word. You can use it to find anything you need.

# Chapter 3 Using a Library

## Words to Know

| | |
|---|---|
| **card catalog** | a computerized or index card file that lists books, magazines, CD-ROMs, and other library sources by title, author, subject, and key word |
| **fiction** | imaginary stories, such as novels and short stories |
| **nonfiction** | writings about true-to-life events or subjects |
| **literature** | writings that are imaginative |
| **call number** | the Dewey Decimal number by which a nonfiction book is arranged on a library shelf |
| **Dewey Decimal System** | a system of numbering library books |
| **reference section** | a section of a library containing the most-used books of information |
| **almanac** | a book published each year that lists many facts, statistics, and other kinds of information |
| **atlas** | a book that contains maps of regions, countries, and continents |
| **periodicals** | magazines, newspapers, and journals |

## Riddle Project

Write a "What Am I?" riddle about five of the items you might find in a library. For example, you might write the following riddle about fiction: *I am written from the world of novels and short stories. Some people call me literature. What am I?* Then trade papers with a partner to see if you can answer each other's riddles.

## Learning Objectives

- Identify three reasons to use a library.
- Use a computerized or paper card catalog.
- Find books shelved by the Dewey Decimal System.
- Identify four types of reference books.
- Locate information in the *Readers' Guide to Periodical Literature.*

## SKILL 3.1 Use a Library

A library contains information on just about everything. You can find a book on how to be more popular. You can find a fitness magazine or video with advice on how to strengthen your back. A good novel can take you to a land of coconuts and palm trees. With good English skills, you can use a library to help you with almost all your needs.

Why should you bother using a library? Here are some of a library's most important features.

- There is no charge for borrowing library books.
- A library is set up to help you find what you need quickly and easily. Librarians are always on duty to help you with special requests.
- A library has books, magazines, newspapers, CDs, CD-ROMs, and possibly even the Internet to serve people with different interests and reading skills.
- A library is part of your community. Besides finding books, magazines, and other materials in it, you can find out about many community services. Information found in libraries can help you do your taxes or find a job. Some libraries even have programs to help improve your reading skills.

## Practice

Use a separate sheet of paper to answer these questions.

1. What are three reasons for using a library?

2. Think about any visit you made to a library. What did you go there to find? How did you go about finding it?

## SKILL 3.2 Use a Card Catalog

You have gone to a library to find a book on job hunting. Also, a friend has asked you to pick up a book about her favorite sports star. A **card catalog**, or file that lists books, magazines, CD-ROMs, and other library resources, can help you find both of the books you need.

A card catalog is either on computer or in a set of small file drawers with cards in them. You can look up books by subject headings, such as "pilot" or "careers." You can also look up books by the author's last name. You can look up books by the title of the book.

On a computerized card catalog, you can search for a specific author or title. You can also browse, or look through, the subjects. If you do not have a specific author, title, or subject, you can often search the catalog by entering key words, such as "pilot" and "job hunting."

**English and Technology**

Many libraries have put their card catalogs onto a computer. Would you rather use an index card file or a computer to search for library information? Tell why in two sentences.

## Practice

Use a separate sheet of paper to write the answers to these questions.

1. You want to find a book about collies, a special breed of dog. What are two subject headings you might look under in a card catalog?

2. You want to read a book by Dave Lancaster. What would you look under in a card catalog?

3. You want to find a video about how to prepare for moving day. What three key words could you enter to search a computerized card catalog?

### What Is on the Card?

The cards in an index card catalog or the screens on a computerized card catalog tell you a little bit about each book. Look at the screen below.

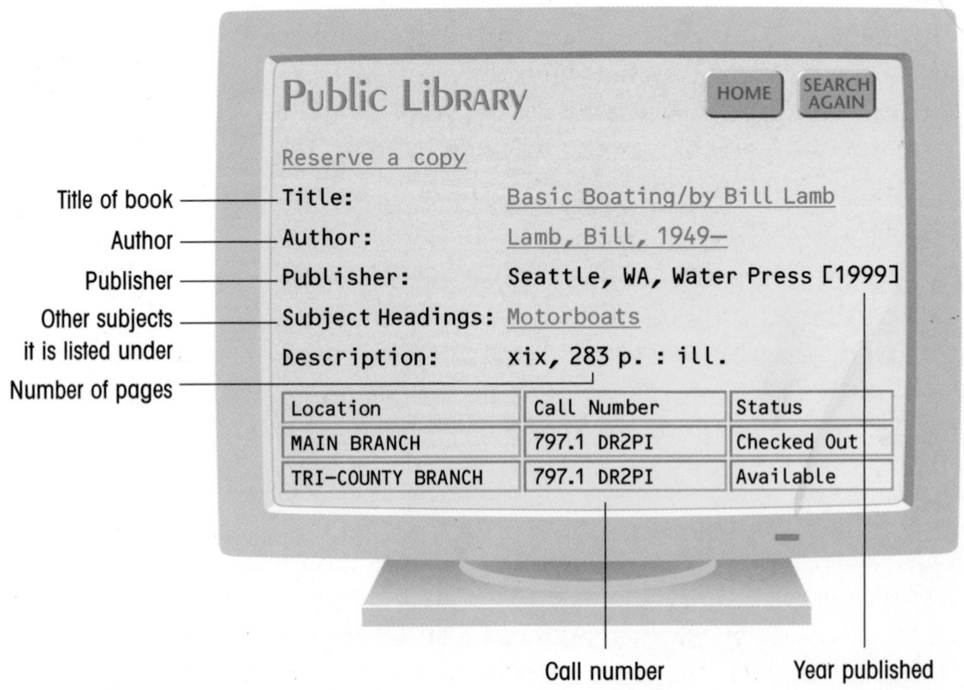

## Practice

Use the computerized entry from a card catalog on page 34 to answer the following questions. Write your answers on a separate sheet of paper.

1. What is the title of the book?
2. Who wrote it?
3. How many pages does it have?
4. Could you use this book to find information about a speedboat built in 2000? Explain your answer.
5. What other subjects could you look under in the card catalog to find books on the same subject?

## SKILL 3.3 Locate Fiction and Nonfiction

The card or computerized entry in a card catalog can also tell you if a book is **fiction** or **nonfiction.** Fiction is imaginary stories such as novels and short stories. **Literature,** or writings that are imaginative, is fiction. Nonfiction is writings about true-to-life events or subjects.

To tell whether a book is listed as fiction or nonfiction, look at the top left side of the card or screen. If a book is fiction, you will see "F" or "Fiction." To find fiction, you need to go to the *Fiction* section of a library. The books are in alphabetical order by each author's last name.

A card or computerized entry for a nonfiction book will have a **call number.** This call number is part of the **Dewey Decimal System,** a system of numbering library books. The Dewey Decimal System organizes books into different subject areas. For example, the call number for books about health care might begin with 616.

### Everyday English

Which do you like to read better, fiction or nonfiction? Would you choose to read a made-up story about detectives or an article on how to become a detective? Why?

**English Tip**
The shelves of the library are often called *stacks.*

Nonfiction books are placed on the shelves in the order of their call numbers. A book with the call number 808.52 would be on the shelf before 808.53. A book with the call number 705.06 would be on the shelf before 705.14.

## Practice

On a separate sheet of paper, put the following call numbers in order. Start with the lowest number.

| | | |
|---|---|---|
| 843.1 | 983.24 | 123.354 |
| 933.1 | 256.34 | 934.25 |
| 842 | 395.93 | 732.14 |

### The Reference Section

Sometimes, you will find "R," "Ref," or "Reference" in front of a call number. This tells you that the book you are looking for is in the **reference section** of the library.

A library's most-used books of information are in the reference section. Because they are used so much, these books cannot be checked out. Four of the most important kinds of reference books are dictionaries, encyclopedias, almanacs, and atlases.

## SKILL 3.4 Use a Dictionary

Dictionaries contain most of the words in the English language and their meanings. They also tell what part of speech each word is (noun, verb, and so on). They explain how each word is pronounced and some give examples of how a word can be used in a sentence. Some dictionaries even tell the origin of the word, or what language it came from. Besides looking up word meanings, a dictionary is a good place to check your spelling.

**Brush Up on the Basics**

A dictionary usually lists the correct forms of irregular verbs. (See Grammar 24 in the Reference Guide.)

**revise** (re-VĪZ) *verb* to change or alter: I have to *revise* my opinion.

### Practice

Use the dictionary definition above to answer the following questions. Write the answers on a separate sheet of paper.

1. After you *revise* something, is it the same or different?
2. Does *revise* rhyme with *ice* or *eyes*?
3. What part of speech is *revise*?

## SKILL 3.5 Use Other Reference Books

### Everyday English

Some people have poor library manners. They take home books from the reference section. Other people keep library books way past their due date, or never return them at all. Why does this cause problems for other people?

### Encyclopedia

Suppose you need to do a report on the lost continent of Atlantis. An encyclopedia is a good place to start. An encyclopedia gives a summary of information on just about every subject. It is often made up of 10 to 20 books called *volumes*. Subjects are listed alphabetically in each volume. For instance, the subject heading "Atlantis" would be found in the volume labeled "A." Encyclopedias are often available on the Internet or CD-ROM, as well as in regular book form.

### Almanac

An **almanac** is a mini-encyclopedia. Like encyclopedias, almanacs are often available on the Internet or a CD-ROM. They are full of facts. They tell a tiny bit about many subjects. Since most almanacs come out yearly, they contain the most current information. You could use an almanac to find out how much rain falls in Hawaii. You could even use it to find out who won the basketball championship last year.

### Atlas

Are you going on a long road trip? Do you need to do a report on the country of India? An **atlas** can help you. An atlas contains maps of cities, states, countries, and continents. Atlases are often available on the Internet or CD-ROMs.

## Practice

Which reference book would be best to help you find the information below? Choose from the words in the box. Then write a sentence explaining each choice. Write your answers on a separate sheet of paper.

| dictionary | encyclopedia | almanac | atlas |
|---|---|---|---|

1. You need to do a report on armadillos.

2. You are traveling across the country. You want to see which cities you will be going through.

3. You and your friend are having an argument about which country won the most gold medals in the latest Olympics.

4. You want to know what it means to be "compliant."

## SKILL 3.6 Find Articles in Magazines

You want to find out the latest news on sports cars. An encyclopedia does not have the most current information. An almanac tells you who won the Indianapolis 500 last year but nothing else. Can a library help you?

Yes, libraries have the latest issues of many **periodicals,** or magazines, newspapers, and journals. Libraries also have many earlier back issues, or previous, noncurrent issues of periodicals. To find articles listed in these periodicals, you can use the *Readers' Guide to Periodical Literature.* It is usually available in both a computerized format and in book form.

The *Readers' Guide* is found in the reference section of the library. In book form, the *Readers' Guide* is made up of many volumes. Each volume lists magazine articles published during a certain time. For example, you will find something like this in the front of a *Readers' Guide.*

*Includes indexing from October 15 to November 4, 1998*

This tells you that articles published during that time are listed in that volume.

In the *Readers' Guide,* articles are grouped together by subject. The subjects are listed in alphabetical order. To find the latest articles on sports cars, this is what you would do.

1. Find the *Readers' Guide* volume that lists the most recent articles.

2. Look up "Sports Cars."

This is what you would find:

**SPORTS CARS**

Design

The affordable Porsche is axed...but new 944 looks smarter, goes faster. P.O. Bingham and T. Orme. il *Motor Trend* 40:21 O '00

Heavy breather! Corvette ZR1 [cover story] R. Grable. Morgan Plus Four turns sweet 16. M. Cotton. il *Motor Trend* 40:19 O '00

History

25 years of greatness [Porsche 911] J. Karr. il *Motor Trend* 40:96-8+ O '00

Happy birthday, Corvette! [cover story] C. Gromer and B. Erdman. il *Popular Mechanics* 165:58-60+ S '00

Testing

Chevrolet Corvette ZR1 [cover story] C. Csere. il *Car and Driver* 34:38-42 O '00

Ferrari F40 at Pista di Fiorano. D. Fuller. il *Motor Trend* 40:108-15 O '00

New toys for mom and dad [Buick Reatta, Ford Probe, Honda CRX, Mazda RX-7] D. Chaikin. il *Home Mechanix* 84:78-83+ O '00

That was then, this is now [Corvettes] R. Taylor. il *Popular Mechanics* 165:64-5+ S '00

### What the *Readers' Guide* Tells You

Look at the listings under "Sports Cars." As you can see, the articles are broken down into three smaller groups: Design, History, and Testing.

The labels on the sample entry below explain what information is given about each article.

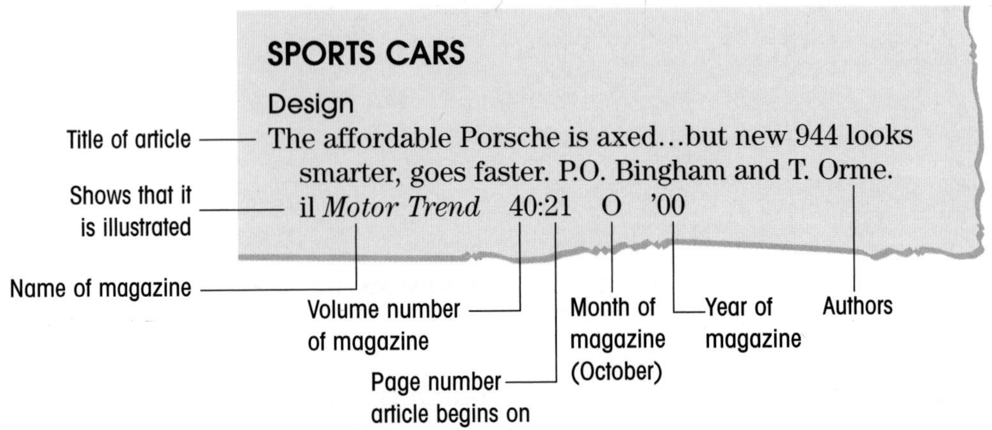


## Practice

Use the sample entry above to answer the following questions. Write your answers on a separate sheet of paper.

1. In which magazine will you find this article?

2. On what page number does the article start?

3. What do you think the article is about?

### The Friendly Librarian

Once you know which magazine you are looking for, how do you find it? Often, libraries list written instructions that tell you what to do. If you need help, you can always ask a librarian.

Librarians can help you use a computerized card catalog system. They can help you think of subject names. They can also help you find reference books. It is their job to help. Don't be afraid to ask for help if you need it.

### Tips on Using the Library

Most libraries are "user friendly." Use these tips to make the most of your library.

1. Libraries often have plenty of signs. They tell you how to use the card catalog, find magazines, and look up newspaper articles. Look for these signs and read them.

2. Ask a librarian for a tour. Get to know the library and its sections.

3. Remember that a library is a community resource. Read bulletin boards to find out about services and opportunities. Have good library manners and return books on time.

4. Always take a notebook and a pen or pencil to a library. Take notes to remember call numbers of books. Write down what you went there to find out!

**English and Careers**

Knowing how to find information is important in places other than a library. Mechanics, for example, sometimes check measurements in repair manuals. What information might you have to look up on a job?

Chapter

# 3 Review

## Summary

| |
|---|
| A library is a place to find free information on many subjects. It is also a good place to find out what is happening in the community. |
| A card catalog is a library user's most important tool. It lists all books by author, title, and subject. Computerized card catalogs also let you search by key word. |
| Nonfiction books are organized with Dewey Decimal System call numbers. Fiction books are usually in a special fiction section. They are organized by the author's last name. |
| A library's most-used books of information are in the reference section. These include dictionaries, encyclopedias, almanacs, and atlases. These books are often also available on the Internet and CD-ROM. |
| Magazine articles can be found by using the *Readers' Guide to Periodical Literature*. |
| A librarian is an important library resource. |

| |
|---|
| periodicals |
| card catalog |
| fiction |
| call number |
| Dewey Decimal System |

## Vocabulary Review

**Complete each sentence with a term from the box. Use a separate sheet of paper.**

1. Nonfiction books are numbered according to the ____.
2. All library books are listed by author, title, and subject in the ____.
3. The number by which a nonfiction book is filed on a library shelf is the ____.
4. Literature such as novels about made-up events is called ____.
5. Magazines, newspapers, and journals are all ____.

## Chapter Quiz

**Answer the following questions in one or two sentences. Use a separate sheet of paper.**

1. What are three good reasons to use a library?
2. What are three ways books are listed in a card catalog?
3. What is a call number?
4. How would you know that a book is fiction by looking at a computerized or an index card entry?
5. How would you know that a book is in the reference section by looking at a card from the card catalog?
6. What are two reasons to use a dictionary?
7. How is an almanac different from an encyclopedia?
8. When might you use an atlas?
9. What is the *Readers' Guide to Periodical Literature*?
10. Why might you look up information in magazines instead of an encyclopedia?

## Critical Thinking

How would you use the index of an atlas? Write your answer on a separate sheet of paper.

### Group Activity

Work with a group of five people to write a series of five letters to the mayor who wants to close down the city library. The letters should explain to the mayor that you do not want the library to be closed. What can your group say in the letters to keep the mayor from closing down the library?

*Taking tests is much easier if you plan ahead of time. It helps to go over your notes with a study partner.*

# Chapter 4 Passing Tests

## Words to Know

| | |
|---|---|
| **objective test** | a test that asks a person to choose one answer over another |
| **short-answer test** | a test that asks a person to write one or two sentences to answer a question |
| **essay test** | a test that asks a person to write at least one paragraph on a certain subject |
| **summarize** | to explain, in writing or speech, the major events or ideas without using details |
| **analyze** | to figure something out; to interpret information |

### Test Project

Write ten questions that you might find on an objective test about this chapter. Write each question on one side of an index card and the answer on the back of the card. Then trade cards with a partner and answer each other's questions.

### Learning Objectives

- Identify three kinds of tests.
- Describe two skills for taking each kind of test.
- Identify at least three resources that help a person prepare for tests.
- Explain at least three study techniques.
- Describe four good study conditions.

## SKILL 4.1 Identify Kinds of Tests

### What Kind of Test Is It?

Usually, you will know ahead of time the kind of test you are preparing for. Perhaps you will be asked to write about a certain subject. Maybe you will be asked to follow written instructions while you perform a job-related task. Knowing what kind of test you are going to take will help you prepare for it. The most common kinds of tests are

- Objective tests
- Short-answer tests
- Essay tests

You need certain skills to take each type of test.

> **English and Careers**
>
> Knowing how to answer different kinds of questions can help you do better during a job interview. What are some objective questions an interviewer might ask you?

### Objective Tests

An **objective test** asks you to choose the right answer from one or more possible answers. Some examples of objective tests are

- True/False
- Multiple-Choice
- Fill in the Blank

The GED (General Education Diploma) Test and many college entrance exams are objective tests. In the GED, you are given a problem or asked to read about a subject. Then you are asked to choose one of four answers given to you.

### Test-Taking Tips

Here are some things to keep in mind when you take an objective test.

1. Read all directions carefully. The directions will tell you how to mark your answers correctly.

2. Notice answers that have *always* or *never* in them. They are usually false.

3. Read questions and answers carefully. A word such as *not, never, except,* or *always* is a key to a sentence's meaning. Missing such a key word may cause you to choose a wrong answer.

4. The first answer you choose is usually the right answer. Unless you are absolutely sure you were wrong, stick with your first choice.

5. You may not know an answer on a multiple-choice test right away. Begin by crossing off the answers that are clearly wrong. When you have narrowed your choices, take a guess. On most objective tests, it is better to answer a question than to leave it blank.

6. If you are having trouble with a particular question, skip it and move on to the next question. Save enough time to go back later to the question you skipped.

**Everyday English**

Written tests are not the only way to find out about a person's knowledge or skills. How else would you measure someone's knowledge in a particular area?

## Practice

Choose the best ending to each of the following sentences. Then explain why you did not choose the other two endings. (Use the *Test-Taking Tips* on page 49 as a model.) Write your answers on a separate sheet of paper.

**1.** Guessing at the answer on an objective test is
   **a.** always the right thing to do.
   **b.** never the right thing to do.
   **c.** usually better than not answering at all.

**2.** On an objective test, it is best to
   **a.** read for key words.
   **b.** never change the first answer you pick.
   **c.** write in ink.

## SKILL 4.2 Take Short-Answer Tests

On some tests you will read the directions below.

*Use no more than two or three sentences to answer each of the following questions.*

These directions let you know that you are about to take a **short-answer test.** The best answers on such a test contain only key information. Answers should be direct and to the point. They should not contain any information that was not asked for. The answers must be written in complete sentences. Look at the two examples on the next page. They give an idea of the right way and the wrong way to write a short answer.

**Everyday English**

What kind of tests are the chapter quizzes in this book?

Question: How are short-answer tests different from objective tests?

### Example 1: Right Way to Write a Short Answer

In most objective tests, the test-taker must choose from a number of given answers. In short-answer tests, the test-taker must come up with the answer independently. The answer must be written in complete sentences.

### Example 2: Wrong Way to Write a Short Answer

Objective tests = make choices. Short answer = write full sentences. I like objective tests more.

## Practice

Explain why Example 2 is **not** the way to write a short answer. On a separate sheet of paper, give examples of what the person did wrong.

## SKILL 4.3 Take Essay Tests

At some time you may be asked to take an **essay test.** Essay tests ask you to write at least one paragraph on a subject. What is the most important thing to keep in mind when you are taking an essay test? Know exactly what you are supposed to write about. Most often, you will be asked to either **summarize** or **analyze** a topic. There is a big difference between these two directions. To summarize a story or article, you write about the major events or ideas. You give only important facts. If you are asked to analyze the article, you go beyond the facts and give your opinion. You interpret information and explain your thinking.

**Brush Up on the Basics**

When you take an essay test, remember to use verbs that agree with their subjects. Using the correct verb form will make your writing clearer. (See Grammar 17–24 in the Reference Guide.)

## Practice

Use a separate sheet of paper to complete these activities.

1. Think about an argument that two of your friends or relatives had. In one paragraph, *summarize* the facts. Answer the *who, what, why, when, where,* and *how* questions. Be sure to write in complete sentences.

2. In the second paragraph, *analyze* the argument. Say who you think was right, and explain your choice.

## SKILL 4.4 Prepare for Tests

You are preparing for a cross-country race. You get the advice of a coach and develop a training schedule. You run a certain number of miles every day. You clock your times. For support, you find other athletes to run with. You help each other train. By race day, you are feeling nervous but confident. You know that you are prepared to do your best.

You can prepare for a test in the same way. To "train" for taking a test, begin by gathering resources. A resource is something you can use to help you. Here are some good "test-training" resources.

- **Test-study books** There are test-study books for the GED, the SAT, government exams, and more. They contain sample tests and study-skill practice. Use your library skills to find the books you need.
- **Classes** There are many classes to help you prepare for the GED and other exams. These classes are often costly, but sometimes your school or a community college will offer them at a low price.

- **Internet** There are also many Internet Web sites that can help you prepare for exams. Sometimes there is a fee for using these sites, but many offer advice, strategies, and practice questions for free.
- **Textbooks** Usually, you will be studying from a textbook such as this one. Take notes and organize the material that will be on the test, using chapter headings.
- **A dictionary** Keep this important reference book handy while you study.
- **A study partner** You can help each other by discussing what you read and by asking each other questions about it.

### Tips for Studying

How can you make the most of your study time? Here are some tips to help you.

1. Start studying well before test time. Do not wait until the last minute.
2. People remember more if they study for short periods each day. Try studying for one hour a day.
3. Study when you feel alert and fresh. Many people feel better in the early morning or late at night. Study in a quiet place.

**English Tip**
Listen to your body. What time of the day is best for you to study? Why?

## Practice

On a separate sheet of paper, write five examples of your own best study conditions. Think about the time of day and the clothing you wear.

Chapter

# 4 Review

## Summary

| |
|---|
| Tests are part of everyday life. Passing tests is often a way to a better job or education. |
| Three common kinds of tests are objective tests, short-answer tests, and essay tests. Each test requires a certain set of skills. |
| There are many resources you can use to help you study for tests. |
| Good study habits will help prepare you for tests. |

| |
|---|
| analyze |
| essay test |
| objective test |
| short-answer test |
| summarize |

## Vocabulary Review

**Complete each sentence with a term from the box. Use a separate sheet of paper.**

1. A test that asks you to write at least a paragraph is an ____.
2. A multiple-choice test is a kind of ____.
3. To explain the main facts is a way to ____.
4. To interpret information is to ____.
5. A test that asks a person to write one or two sentences to answer a question is a ____.

## Chapter Quiz

**Answer the following questions in one or two sentences. Use a separate sheet of paper.**

1. What are three situations in which you might have to take a test?
2. What are three examples of objective tests?
3. How can reading carefully help you pass a multiple-choice test?
4. Why are writing skills important for taking short-answer tests?
5. What is an essay test?
6. What is the difference between summarizing and analyzing information?
7. How can a library help you prepare for a test?
8. How can a study partner help you?
9. What are two good study habits?
10. What are three resources you can use to prepare for a test?

## Critical Thinking

What procedure should you follow when you are not sure of an answer on a multiple-choice test? Write down the procedure in step-by-step order.

### Group Activity

Work with a group to write a fifteen-question test about this chapter. Be sure to include objective questions, short-answer questions, and at least one essay question. Work together to find the answers to the test. Then ask another group to answer the questions.

# Unit 1 Review

**Read each sentence below. Then choose the letter that best completes each one.**

**1.** It is important to take good notes because

A. they take the place of studying.
B. they make it easier to remember things.
C. they make things more difficult.
D. none of the above

**2.** Notes for school are most useful if you study them

A. every day.
B. once a week.
C. only the night before a test.
D. never.

**3.** The part of a book that is like a small dictionary is the

A. index.
B. table of contents.
C. glossary.
D. caption.

**4.** The appendix is found in the

A. front of the book.
B. middle of the book.
C. first chapter of the book.
D. back of the book.

**5.** An example of a periodical is

A. an encyclopedia.
B. a fiction book.
C. a magazine.
D. an atlas.

**6.** Almanacs can be found in the section of the library called

A. reference.
B. fiction.
C. nonfiction.
D. none of the above

**7.** A multiple-choice test is an example of

A. an essay test.
B. an objective test.
C. a short-answer test.
D. a subjective test.

**8.** Answers that have "never" in them are

A. usually true.
B. usually false.
C. always true.
D. always false.

**Critical Thinking**

How is preparing for a test like preparing for an athletic contest? Name three ways.

**WRITING** Write a short essay explaining how preparing for a test is like preparing for an athletic contest. Your essay should be at least three paragraphs long.

Unit 2

# English for Smart Shopping

*Advertising has a lot of influence on the decisions we make. Practical English skills help you make wise decisions.*

# Chapter 5 English Skills and Advertising

## Words to Know

| | |
|---|---|
| **ad copy** | spoken or written words in advertising |
| **consumer** | a person who buys goods and services |
| **fact** | information that can be measured or proved as true |
| **evidence** | proof; statements that back up a claim that something is true |
| **opinion** | information based on a person's experience or thoughts; not a fact |
| **emotions** | feelings |
| **comparative** | a word used when saying how two things are alike or different |

## Advertisement Project

Think of a new item that could be sold in a school store. Describe what the product can do and why students should buy it. Give your product a name. Then create an advertisement for your school newspaper about the new product.

## Learning Objectives

- Explain three reasons to analyze ads.
- Locate facts and opinions in ads.
- Identify misleading words in ads and explain how they are used.
- Use note-taking and letter-writing skills to make effective complaints.

**English and Careers**

People who write ad copy often begin by filling out a fact sheet on a product. They include the most important facts in what they write.

Spoken or written words in advertising are called **ad copy.** Ad copy is aimed at getting you, the **consumer,** to buy something. By using some English skills, you can analyze any ad copy. Analyzing ad copy can help you

- know how truthful an ad is.
- decide how good a product or service is.
- save money.

## SKILL 5.1 Identify Facts and Opinions

Ad copy usually contains two kinds of information. One kind is fact and the other is opinion.

A **fact** is a piece of information that can be measured or proved. Facts are usually proved with **evidence,** or more information to show that they are true. Suppose you saw a sign showing a smiling woman holding lots of cash. The words "Save Big at Jolly Stores" are at the bottom of the sign. Is there any evidence to back up that statement?

The ad gives no real evidence that you will save money at Jolly Stores. At this point, the ad copy is only an **opinion.** An opinion is an idea that other people can agree or disagree with. Opinions often come from a person's own experience, values, or thoughts.

When you read or listen to ads, analyze them for facts and opinions. Look for evidence. A list of low prices at Jolly stores would be one kind of evidence to support the opinion that you will save money at Jolly stores.

## Practice

Read and analyze the following ad copy. On a separate sheet of paper, list the facts, evidence, and opinions in each ad. Then write whether it would be wise to buy the product based on the ad.

1. Use Nature Glo shampoo. It leaves your hair healthy and alive!

2. Hamburger Heaven has the best-selling hamburgers in the state. We sell 17,000 burgers a day. You'll love them, too!

## SKILL 5.2 Write Ad Copy

You are going to buy a new pair of jeans. One pair of jeans is advertised as "slim and slinky." The other pair is advertised as "long-lasting." Based on those words, which would you buy? Why?

> **Everyday English**
>
> More than $75 billion is spent each year in the United States on advertising.

### Using Words to Suit Your Purpose

Words are powerful tools. Ad writers know that certain kinds of words will appeal to different kinds of people. The "slim and slinky" jeans will probably appeal to the **emotions**, or feelings, of young people. The "long-lasting" jeans will probably appeal to the emotions of people who are careful about spending money.

Unfortunately, words can be misleading. Watch out for misleading words when you analyze ads.

**Brush Up on the Basics**

Many misleading words are adjectives. An adjective describes a noun—a person, place, thing, event, or idea. (See Grammar 34–38 in the Reference Guide.)

### Misleading Words

A shopper picks up a box of cereal. On the front, it says "Natural." That sounds healthy, but being a smart shopper, the shopper reads the box more closely. The cereal is natural. There are no added chemicals. However, it has hardly any vitamins or nutrients in it. The word *natural* is misleading. When you see it, you think you are getting a healthy food.

When you read an ad, you should watch for misleading words. Such words are usually used to describe the product or what it can do. *New, fresh, natural, healthy, light,* and *improved* are examples of words that can be misleading. Look for evidence to back up the words. Only then should you take the ad seriously.

## Practice

Use a separate sheet of paper to answer these questions. Write two or three sentences for each answer.

1. A brand of milk is called "Always Fresh." Are these words misleading? Explain your answer.

2. A magazine ad has a picture of a car. Under the picture are these words: *An amazing car for amazing people.* Which words in the ad appeal to the emotions? Explain how the words could be misleading.

### More Misleading Words

"Get your clothes *brighter* and *whiter.*"

"X-300 engine . . . *more powerful*"

"*Prettier* eyes with Black Lash Makeup"

Each line of ad copy above uses a kind of word called a **comparative.** A comparative shows how two things are alike or different. The people who wrote the ad copy above did not say what they were comparing. Are the clothes brighter and whiter than clothes washed in plain water? Is the X-300 engine more powerful than a turtle? How will your eyes be prettier? Whenever you see a comparative, ask yourself, *"What is being compared?"* When you use a comparative, be sure to point out the two things you are comparing.

> **Everyday English**
>
> Do you believe everything you read or see in ads? Why or why not?

## Practice

Write your own ad copy using the comparatives below. Make sure you include the two things you are comparing. Use a separate sheet of paper.

1. more exciting
2. funnier
3. better than

## SKILL 5.3 Complain About Ads

Let's face it. Ads are not always 100% truthful. Ads can show cartoon characters selling toothpaste. Ads can show people flying in outer space. Sometimes ads even tell lies. Perhaps they advertise a wrong price, or maybe they show a product doing something it cannot do. As a consumer, you can complain about these ads. The state and federal governments have agencies to stop false advertising. You can find their numbers listed under "Consumer Protection" in the white pages of a telephone book. You can also look under other government agency listings.

### Notes for Being Heard

**English Tip**
Remember to use a firm but polite tone when you complain. Often the person to whom you are speaking will pass your complaint on to another person who can make a decision about your complaint.

Before you complain, make notes about what you are going to say. Your notes should provide the information below.

- Who you are
- What you are complaining about
- Where you saw the ad
- When you saw it
- Why you think it is false
- How you found out it was false

You can complain in person, by telephone, or in a letter. When you complain in person, stay calm. State your case clearly. Ask for action. If you do not get help, ask to speak to another person.

If you complain in a letter, use the example on the next page as a model.

111 A Street — Your address
Hatter, North Carolina 55589
September 1, 2000 — The date

Consumer Complaints
False Advertising Division — The Department or Agency you are writing to.
Raleigh, North Carolina 55599

Dear Consumer Complaints: — The greeting

I am writing to complain about a false ad. The ad appeared in the <u>City News</u> on August 15 of this year. It stated that our local Jolly Store was having a storewide sale. When I went to the Jolly Store, I found only a few items on sale.

I believe this ad is false and should not be allowed to run. Please let me know what you can do about it.

— The body of the letter explains why you are writing, what happened, and what you expect.

Very truly yours, — The closing

*Joe Jones* — Your signature

Joe Jones — Your name (typed or printed)

## Practice

A newspaper ad said CDs were on sale at Soundland for $10.99. When you got there, there were no $10.99 CDs. The salesperson told you that those CDs were poor quality anyway. He then tried to sell you CDs for $15.99. The date was June 16th of this year.

Write a letter complaining about this false ad. Use the model above. Write your letter on a separate sheet of paper.

Chapter

# 5 Review

## Summary

Ads are designed to get you to buy products or services. Analyzing ad copy can help you make smart buys.

Begin to analyze ads by looking at facts and opinions. Facts should be backed up by evidence.

Look for misleading words such as "new and improved." Again, look for evidence to back up these words.

Ad copy often uses comparative words without really comparing two things. This can be misleading.

Note-taking and letter-writing skills can help you make effective complaints about ads.

| ad copy |
|---|
| consumer |
| fact |
| opinion |
| comparative |

## Vocabulary Review

**Match each term in the box with its meaning. Write the term and its matching number on a separate sheet of paper.**

1. a person who buys goods and services
2. information that can be proved as true
3. a word used to compare two things
4. words written or spoken in ads
5. information based on thoughts or experience

## Chapter Quiz

**Answer the following questions in one or two sentences. Use a separate sheet of paper.**

1. What are three reasons to analyze ads?
2. What is the difference between a fact and an opinion? Give an example of each.
3. What is an example of ad copy that contains a fact?
4. What is an example of ad copy that contains an opinion?
5. Why might the word "natural" be misleading?
6. What is a comparative? Give an example.
7. A soap is advertised as having a "cleaner smell." Rewrite the ad copy so that you know what is being compared.
8. What makes an ad false?
9. How would you find the agency to complain to about false advertising?

## Critical Thinking

You want to learn more about the laws governing advertising. What three subject headings could you look under in the card catalog of a library?

## Group Activity

Work with a group to discuss some ads you have all seen on television. Which ad does your group think is the best? Which ad does your group think is the worst? Discuss your choices. Then design two awards—one for the best ad and one for the worst ad. Write a short group paragraph explaining your choices.

*Careful shoppers do more than compare prices. They know what they are buying and make decisions based on their values.*

Chapter 6

# English Skills for Buying

## Words to Know

| | |
|---|---|
| **product** | something for sale that has been manufactured or grown |
| **service** | a skill that a person offers, such as washing a car |
| **pros** | reasons for; in favor of |
| **cons** | reasons against |
| **service contract** | a written agreement to provide a service |
| **warranty** | a guarantee on a product or service |
| **estimate** | a guess at what something will cost |
| **reference** | a person who can say whether a product or service is good or poor |

## Buying Project

Think of something you would like to buy. Use the *Who, What, Why, Where, When,* and *How* questions to create a question guide about that item. Then go to the library or use the Internet to find answers to your questions. When you have answered all your questions, decide whether you still want to buy the item.

## Learning Objectives

- Describe three steps used in making good buys.
- Use reading and library skills to build a "buyer's vocabulary."
- Make a question guide for getting information about products and services.
- Explain pros and cons to help make buying decisions.

**Brush Up on the Basics**

Remember to use a period (.) after a declarative sentence and a question mark (?) after an interrogative sentence. (See Punctuation 1 in the Reference Guide.)

Being a good consumer means being a careful consumer. You can get the **products** and **services** that match your needs if you understand the steps for making a good buy. You can be happy with what you pay for, and that is really what being a smart buyer is all about.

## SKILL 6.1 Gather Key Information

### Three Steps to a Good Buy

To make a good buy, use these three steps.

1. Gather information about what you want to buy.

This can be as simple as reading labels, or it can mean reading magazine articles, talking to people, and taking notes. Most of the time, you will gather information on two or more similar products or services so you can compare them.

2. List the pros and cons for making your purchase.

List the **pros,** or reasons for, and **cons,** or reasons against, buying at least two products or services. This will help you compare them. Look at the good and bad features of each thing. This way, you will know exactly what you would be paying for.

3. Make a decision based on your values.

Your values are the things that are important to you. Some people think that saving money is the most important thing. Others do not care how much they pay, as long as they are happy with the quality of the goods or services they buy.

## Practice

Write two or three sentences about something you paid for and were unhappy with. Include one lesson you learned from that experience.

### Key Information

Begin by finding key information. Key information is found on labels and packages. It is found in product booklets. It can also be found in a **service contract**, or written agreement to provide a service.

Here are some examples of key information found on labels. Suppose you are concerned about your weight. You go into a store to buy bread. You read on the label that one slice of Brand X bread contains 100 calories and 4 grams of fat. One slice of Brand Y contains 80 calories and 1 gram of fat. You now have key information to make your buying decision.

> **Everyday English**
>
> You do not like the taste of Brand Y bread. Is it still worth buying? Explain.

### Words for Buying

How much key information you gather depends on what you are buying. For clothing, food, and other small items, you may want to read only package labels. For big purchases, you will want to read sales information. You will want to talk to people who know about what you are buying. You will probably want to read articles in consumer books and magazines. To make sense of this information, you will have to build a "buyer's vocabulary." Here are some examples of words and phrases that might be useful.

**As Is:** This usually means there is something wrong with what you are thinking of buying. Perhaps a piece of clothing is stained or torn. Perhaps a piece of furniture is scratched. Look closely at items that are marked "As Is." They usually cannot be returned.

**Bait and Switch:** Stores sometimes advertise an item at a low price. However, when the buyer asks for the item, the store does not have it in stock. The salesperson will try to sell the buyer a more expensive item. This practice is called "bait and switch." It is against the law.

**Care Manual:** Most products come with a care manual. This manual will help the buyer learn how to operate and take care of the item.

**English Tip**
As you read, make a list of unfamiliar words in a full or limited warranty. Then look up the words in a dictionary to be sure you understand everything your warranty covers.

**Full Warranty:** A **warranty** is a guarantee that a product or service is good. Full warranties *usually* cover the cost of all parts and labor for a certain period of time so you do not have to pay for them.

**Labor:** This refers to work done to repair an item.

**Limited Warranty:** A warranty covers only *some* costs or kinds of repairs on an item. The buyer must read limited warranties carefully to know just what is covered.

**RDA:** This abbreviation stands for *recommended daily allowance*. RDA tells what percentage of recommended daily vitamins you are getting in a serving of food.

**Service Contract:** This is "repair" insurance for an item. For example, a consumer buys a stereo. The store offers to sell him a service contract for $100. The service contract states that, for one year, the store will fix or replace the stereo at no cost to the customer. Buying a service contract is like buying a limited warranty. Read it carefully.

**Unit Pricing:** This method lets you know exactly how much of a product you are getting for your money. Unit pricing is most often done with foods in grocery stores. Small labels on the shelves below products spell out the "price per unit." A unit may be an ounce, a pound, or any measure.

**English and Technology**

Many packages list one or more company Web site addresses. You can find more information about products at these Web sites and even send an e-mail with a question.

**Example:**

You see two boxes of cereal. Brand A costs $3.29 and weighs 24 ounces. Brand B costs $3.10 and weighs 16 ounces. Which box of cereal gives you the best value?

Brand A Unit Price = 14 cents per ounce

Brand B Unit Price = 19 cents per ounce

Brand A is a better buy.

## Practice

1. A cereal box says that a one-ounce serving of the cereal without milk has 25% of the RDA of Vitamin A. What does that mean?

2. A piece of clothing is labeled "As Is." What does that mean?

3. What kinds of key information should you look for in a limited warranty?

### Ways to Build a Buyer's Vocabulary

Your English skills from Unit 1 can help you build your own buyer's vocabulary. For example, a cereal box contains riboflavin. What is riboflavin? Look it up in a dictionary. Do you want to know more about it? Look it up in an encyclopedia or on the Internet. Do you want to know more about nutrition in general? Look up "Nutrition" in the card catalog, or do a search on the Internet. Soon a whole new vocabulary about health will be yours.

Sometimes, certain words will not be in a reference book. Suppose you want to know what "digital audio sound" means. You may need to read a current magazine article about stereos. Where will you find such an article? Look in the *Readers' Guide to Periodical Literature* under "Stereos" or do an Internet search.

**Everyday English**

What key information can you find on clothing labels?

Gathering information does not stop at building vocabulary. Consumer books and magazines compare the features of hundreds of products. Look them up in your library. Then use the index, glossary, charts, and graphs to find what you need.

## Practice

Use a separate sheet of paper to answer these questions. Write two or three sentences for each answer. Review the skills you learned in Unit 1 for ideas.

1. The cholesterol amount is sometimes listed on food labels. Sam wants to know what *cholesterol* is. What are two reference books he can use to find out?

2. Diane's doctor tells her that she is allergic to synthetic clothing. What reference book might give her a list of synthetic fabrics?

3. Todd's friend Jared says Todd's new car must have fuel injection. Jared does not explain what fuel injection is. Todd gets a book on cars. In what part of the book should Todd look for a definition of *fuel injection*?

4. What part of the book would Todd use to see if there is a whole chapter on fuel injection?

### Make a Question Guide

Another useful way to gather information is to ask questions and take notes. Begin by making up a question guide. The question guide should contain the *who, what, why, where, when,* and *how* questions. Suppose you are looking for an auto body shop to repair your car. You will probably take the car into at least two shops for **estimates**, or good guesses at what something costs. Your question guide will help you compare exactly what you will get for each price. Here is an example of a question guide.

1. What does the estimate include? If the actual work costs more, will I have to pay it?
2. Who else have you done work for? Can I get **references**, or the names of people who can say whether a product or service is good or poor?
3. When can you do the work?
4. How long will the repairs take?
5. What kind of warranty do you give?
6. What if I am not satisfied? Will you charge me more for repairing what is still wrong with the car?
7. Where do you get your parts? Are they new or used?

## Practice

You want to join a health club. Make a question guide for information you want to know. Write the questions on a separate sheet of paper.

## SKILL 6.2 List Pros and Cons

Once you have gathered your information, what do you do with it? Make a list, dividing the information into pros and cons. Such a list will help you compare two or more things easily.

Here are the pros and cons for joining two health clubs.

### Health Club One

| Pros | Cons |
|---|---|
| 1. New equipment | 1. No public parking |
| 2. Good trainers | 2. Short hours |
| 3. Nice locker room | 3. Crowded |
| 4. Close to my work | 4. No swimming pool |
| 5. Costs less than Health Club Two | |

### Health Club Two

| Pros | Cons |
|---|---|
| 1. New equipment | 1. Locker room has mold |
| 2. Good trainers | 2. Costs $100 more than Health Club One |
| 3. Swimming pool | 3. Crowded |
| 4. Free parking | |
| 5. Open long hours | |

## Practice

Think of two restaurants you like. List at least two pros and cons for each on a separate sheet of paper.

## SKILL 6.3 Look at Your Values

Once you have listed pros and cons, you need to think about your values. Values are the things that are most important to you. Think back to the health club example. If saving money is very important to you, then you will probably go with Health Club One. But what if you really enjoy swimming? Then you might pay the extra money for Health Club Two. Whatever your choice, you know that what you are getting is close to what you want. That is the key to being a good buyer.

**Everyday English**

Another word for pro is favorable. What is another word for con?

## Practice

Use a separate sheet of paper to answer these questions.

1. Look back at the pros and cons on page 76. Which health club would you choose, and why?

2. Look at your pros and cons for restaurants in the Practice above. Which restaurant do you think is better, and why? What does your choice say about your values?

Chapter

# 6 Review

## Summary

| |
|---|
| English skills can help you be a smart consumer. |
| To get the best buy, gather information. List pros and cons. Then use your values to make a final decision. |
| Gather key information. Use labels, books, and magazines. Reference books, a library, and the Internet can help you build a buyer's vocabulary. |
| A question guide of *who, what, why, where, when,* and *how* questions can be used to get key information. Take notes to compare what you find. |

| |
|---|
| warranty |
| product |
| service |
| pros |
| cons |
| estimate |
| reference |

## Vocabulary Review

**Match each term in the box with its meaning. Write the term and its matching number on a separate sheet of paper.**

1. reasons for doing something
2. a person who can say whether a product or service is good or poor
3. a guess at what something will cost
4. a guarantee
5. something for sale that has been manufactured or grown
6. a skill that is offered
7. reasons against doing something

## Chapter Quiz

**Answer the following questions in one or two sentences. Use a separate sheet of paper.**

1. What are three good reasons for being a smart buyer?
2. What are three steps in smart buying?
3. Where will you find key information on food and on clothing? Give an example of each.
4. You are shopping for stereo speakers. The salesperson says Brand X speakers have the best *woofers* around. How can you find out what woofers are?
5. How can you find out more about Brand X's woofers compared to other brands?
6. What is a question guide, and how can it help you?
7. What are pros and cons?

## Critical Thinking

You are unhappy with a product or service. How could you use a library or the Internet to find out where to complain?

## Group Activity

Work with a group of three to perform a scene between a salesperson in an appliance store and two customers looking to buy a new stereo. One customer has a question guide. The other customer does not. How are their shopping experiences different?

# Unit 2 Review

**Read each sentence below. Then choose the letter that best completes each one.**

**1.** The following lines of ad copy are based on opinion, except

A. Spencer's: the Best Ice Cream!

B. Spencer's: We Sell 20 Gallons of Vanilla Ice Cream Every Week!

C. Spencer's: Your Kids Will Love It!

D. Spencer's Ice Cream Is the Creamiest!

**2.** An opinion is

A. always true.

B. based on a person's experience or thoughts.

C. sometimes also a fact.

D. a kind of statement companies never use in advertisements.

**3.** A letter of complaint about a misleading ad should tell

A. who you are.

B. why you think the ad is false.

C. where you saw the ad.

D. all of the above

**4.** To make a good buy,

A. trust the salesperson to tell you everything you need to know.

B. list pros and cons for yourself before you decide what to buy.

C. read only advertising about the product.

D. do not worry about comparing products.

**5.** A limited warranty is

A. a warranty that covers only some costs or kinds of repairs on an item.

B. credit information a consumer gives to a store.

C. a guarantee that a company will fix any problem you have with a product at no cost.

D. an agreement that a customer will return a product borrowed from a store.

**6.** Before having your car repaired, it is important to get

A. a tour of the repair shop.

B. estimates from at least two shops to find the best price and value.

C. a handshake from the lead mechanic.

D. none of the above

**Critical Thinking**

How do your values affect the way you spend your money? Name two values that are important to you when you buy a new shirt or blouse.

**WRITING** Write a short essay explaining how to get information about products and services. Give an example from your own life. Your essay should be at least three paragraphs long.

Unit 3

# English for Work

Chapter 7
## Job Hunting

Chapter 8
## Applying for a Job

Chapter 9
## Interviewing

Chapter 10
## Beginning Work

Chapter 11
## Learning Job Skills

Chapter 12
## Communicating at Work

*Newspaper "Want Ads," supermarket bulletin boards, Internet bulletin boards, and job placement Web sites are good sources of job listings.*

# Chapter 7 Job Hunting

## Words to Know

| | |
|---|---|
| **goals** | the things a person wants to achieve |
| **interests** | concerns or hobbies |
| **network** | the people you contact to help you get information about jobs |
| **fee** | money charged for a service |
| **editing** | improving writing by making changes |

## "Work Wanted" Project

Use a self-interview guide to determine what kind of work you want to do. Then write an ad for yourself that you could place in a "Work Wanted" section of a newspaper. Remember to write the ad in full sentences for the first draft and then edit it.

## Learning Objectives

- Develop an interview guide to learn about goals, interests, and jobs.
- Use networking for job contacts.
- Scan a bulletin board for job information.
- Identify three ways a telephone book can help with job hunting.
- Locate appropriate jobs in the "Want Ads."
- Write and edit a "Work Wanted" ad.

## SKILL 7.1 Develop an Interview Guide

Everyone has different goals and interests when it comes to work. A construction worker might have to do hard, dirty work. A strong person who likes to work outdoors may enjoy the job. A child-care worker may make only $5.15 per hour but loves working with children. The money is not the most important thing to him. The best jobs are the ones that match your goals and interests.

> **Everyday English**
>
> How do you think reading and thinking skills can help you find a job?

The first task in job hunting is to figure out your own **goals** and **interests.** Goals are things you want to achieve. If you want to make $50,000 a year, that is a goal. If you want to own a restaurant, that is a goal. Interests are things that are important to you, or things that you are curious about. You may have interests in computers or in keeping parks beautiful. Knowing your own interests can lead you to meaningful work.

How do you discover your goals and interests? Interview yourself. Begin by using your English skills to write a self-interview guide. Interview guides begin with those familiar words: *who, what, why, where, when,* and *how.* Here is an example of one person's self-interview guide.

### Self-Interview Guide

1. What skills do I already have? What do I know how to do?

2. What are the things I most like to do?

3. What are skills I would like to learn?

4. Why do I want a job? Am I willing to work for less money now, while I can learn skills that will help me later?

5. Where would I like to work? In a building or outside? In what part of the city?

6. When can I work? Do I need to work certain hours? Will a midnight shift do?

Once you answer these questions, begin to analyze yourself. Are you an outgoing, friendly person, or do you like to work alone? Are you good with machines? Do you like to work with your hands? Would you be happiest sitting at a desk or moving around? As you answer these questions, you will get to know yourself better. You will have a better idea of what kind of job to look for.

**English and Careers**

Some employers give interest tests. These tests have no right or wrong answers. They are designed to help you learn what your interests are.

## Practice

On a separate sheet of paper, make up your own interview guide. Begin with questions from the example and add at least two questions of your own. Then answer the questions.

## SKILL 7.2 Try Several Methods for Job Hunting

Once you know your goals and interests, how do you find a job? There are many resources available to you, including employment agencies, "Want Ads" in newspapers, and Internet Web sites for job placement. There are signs in windows and people with leads. Other workers can also give you information. A few English skills can help you use these resources effectively.

### Method 1: Networking

**English Tip**
Make notes for yourself after you network with someone. Write down the name of the person you spoke with and the place where the person works.

How do you form **networks** with people? Making a network means meeting people, learning about jobs, and getting leads. You begin to build a network by meeting people who have the kind of job you think you want. Then you can use interview questions to learn more about the job. If you feel comfortable, ask the person for leads. Here is how Kevin interviewed a server one night when he was out to dinner.

Kevin: *So, how do you like being a server?*

Server: *It's OK. I make good tips.*

Kevin: *May I ask how much?*

Server: *Oh, maybe $50 a night, $80 on the weekends.*

Kevin: *What don't you like about your job?*

Server: *The hours. You make the best money working weekend nights. That doesn't leave much time for dating. And my feet hurt almost all the time. It's hard work.*

Kevin: *What kind of skills do servers need?*

Server: *You need to be patient. Some customers can really be rude. You need to have good balance so you can carry trays. Of course, you've got to have a good memory. For taking orders, you know. Oh, and then you have to be able to add up bills. There's a lot to it.*

Kevin: *What are the chances of me getting a job here?*

Server: *I'll let you know when a job opens up. Leave me your name and phone number.*

## Practice

What would it be like to be a teacher? Write an interview guide to find out. Use the *who, what, why where, when,* and *how* words to help you. Ask your favorite teacher for an interview. Take notes on what you find out. Does teaching fit your goals and interests?

### Method 2: Scan for Job Information

In Chapter 2, you practiced scanning headings in books. You can also use your scanning skills to find a job. You can scan store windows for "Help Wanted" and "Now Hiring" signs. You can read neighborhood bulletin boards for jobs. When you see a bulletin board, quickly look over the notices. Look for the words *job, worker, pay,* and *work.* You will probably find some information on an available job.

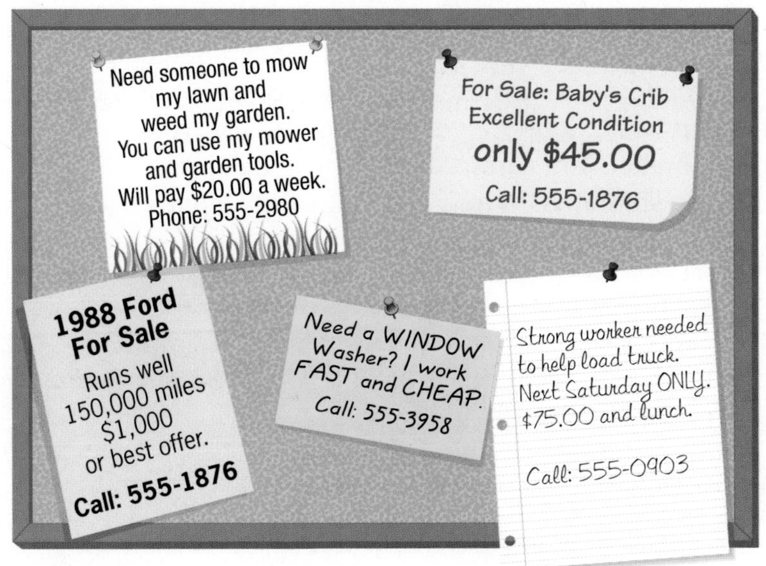

## Practice

Scan the bulletin board on page 87 for jobs. On a separate sheet of paper, write the jobs that are available.

### Method 3: Use the Phone Book

One of the best resources a job hunter has is a phone book. At the front of the white pages, or between the white pages and the yellow pages, is a list of government agencies. These agencies are usually divided into city, county, state, and federal listings. Under each section, you will usually find the heading "Employment" or "Economic Development." Agencies under these headings can help you get training and find jobs. There is usually no charge for using these agencies.

The yellow pages are also helpful for job hunters. You can use the yellow pages to look up private employment agencies. These agencies can test your skills and find work for a **fee**, or money charged for a service. You can also use the yellow pages to find a job in your field. Suppose you are looking for work as a pizza maker. You can look under the headings "Pizza" and "Restaurants." Then you can call the places listed to find out if they have any openings.

## Practice

Use a separate sheet of paper to answer these questions.

1. Jan wants to know if her city has employee training programs. How could she use a telephone book to find out?

2. Pedro would like to find work as an airline flight attendant. What heading could he look under in the yellow pages to find out where to look?

3. What questions could Pedro ask when he calls about the airline job? Develop an interview guide that he could use over the phone. Include at least five questions.

### Method 4: Read the "Want Ads"

One of the best places to look for a job is in the "Help Wanted" section of a newspaper. "Help Wanted" ads are in the "Classified" section.

To put want ads to work for you, follow these steps.

1. Think of at least two possible headings before you start. The job you want may be listed under several headings. For example, if you are looking for a job in sales, you could look under "Salesperson" or "Retail."

2. Scan the "Want Ads" for the job you want. The "Want Ads" are in alphabetical order.

3. Once you find an interesting ad, circle it.

4. Read the ad carefully. Find out what experience you need and how to apply for the job.

**Everyday English**

Does it take the same skills to read the "Want Ads" as it does to read a card catalog? Explain.

## Practice

Do the activities below on a separate sheet of paper.

1. Write the following jobs in alphabetical order: clerk, word processor, sales manager, cashier, accountant.

2. You are looking for a job as a grocery checkout person. Write two headings that you might look under in the "Want Ads."

3. A "Want Ad" says: "Driver and odd jobs for florist. Must know Oakland streets, have neat appearance. 555-3333." Write what skills you might need for this job. Describe how you might prepare for the interview. Write two or three sentences.

### "Want Ad" Abbreviations

Many times, "Want Ads" use abbreviations of words. Read this list of everyday abbreviations and their meanings.

| Abbreviation | Meaning |
|---|---|
| applic. | application (a form you fill out when applying for a job) |
| exp. | experience |
| f/t | full-time (40 hours per week) |
| p/t | part-time (less than 40 hours per week) |
| nec. | necessary (something you must have) |
| pref. | preferred (what the employer would like you to have, though it is not necessary) |
| min. | minimum (the least amount) |
| refs. | references (people who can say what kind of person you are and how good a worker you are) |

| | |
|---|---|
| req. | required (something you must have) |
| temp. | temporary (a job that is for a limited period of time) |
| hrs. | hours |
| wk. | week |
| wkends. | weekends |
| mos. | months |
| yrs. | years |
| / | per (each) |

## Practice

On a separate sheet of paper, write out the following want ad. Use the full word in place of each abbreviation.

**WANTED**

Now hiring counter people p/t and f/t. No exp. nec. Must be at least 16 yrs. old. Work min. of 10 hrs./wk. Pick up applic. at Freddy's, corner of Market and Main.

## SKILL 7.3 Write and Edit "Work Wanted" Ads

Jenny did not have to go out and look for a job. She placed an ad in the "Work Wanted" section of her newspaper. She got several calls a day during the first week.

"I like to hire people who advertise," said one employer. "I know they really want to work."

To write your own ad, you will need to include the following information.

- The kind of job you want
- Your skills and experience
- Where you can be reached
- Whether you want part-time or full-time work
- Any other information you think is important

**Brush Up on the Basics**

Do you remember how to punctuate abbreviations? Remember to use periods (.) after titles and most other shortened forms. (See Punctuation 2 in the Reference Guide.)

Ads usually cost you a certain amount of money per line. For that reason, it is a good idea to write two drafts of your "Want Ad." In the first draft, write whatever you like. Include everything you think is important. Write in full sentences. In the second draft, cut out unnecessary words and information. Use abbreviations. This is called **editing** your work. Take a look at Jenny's first and second drafts for ideas.

**First Draft**

*I am a college student looking for part-time work on nights and weekends. I have child-care skills and a driver's license, and I love children. I do not have a car, though. I have lots of references. Please call me at 555-1211 after 3 P.M. I would like to make at least $6.25 per hour.*

### Edited Version

*Want p/t child-care position on nights and wkends. Exp., driver's license, refs. 555-1211 after 3 P.M. $6.25 per hour.*

## Practice

On a separate sheet of paper, edit the "Work Wanted" ad below. Keep it under 20 words. Abbreviations and phone numbers count as one word each.

**WANTED**

I am looking for work as a typist. I type 90 words per minute. I have worked at a number of offices and have lots of references. I am a good worker. Full-time work is preferred. Call Tom at 555-9990 just about anytime, except Saturdays and Sundays.

Chapter

# 7 Review

## Summary

| |
|---|
| English skills can help you get a job that fits your interests and goals. |
| Interview guides can help you learn about yourself and jobs available in your area. These guides are based on the *who, what, why, where, when,* and *how* questions. |
| Scanning supermarket or Internet bulletin boards lets you quickly find out about available jobs. |
| A phone book can help you find government employment agencies. It can also help you find private employment agencies. You can even use it to find jobs in a certain field. |
| When you read the "Want Ads," know what you are looking for. Look for key information in an ad to help you prepare for a job interview. |
| "Work Wanted" ads can be a good way to find work. They should be brief and to the point. They should use abbreviations. |

| |
|---|
| goals |
| network |
| interests |
| editing |
| fee |

## Vocabulary Review

**Match each term in the box with its meaning. Write the term and its matching number on a separate sheet of paper.**

**1.** the people you contact to help you get information about jobs

**2.** the things a person wants to achieve

**3.** improving writing by making changes

**4.** money charged for a service

**5.** concerns or hobbies

## Chapter Quiz

**Answer the following questions in one or two sentences. Use a separate sheet of paper.**

1. What are two ways to use an interview guide?
2. What are two questions you could ask yourself to discover your interests and goals?
3. What are two examples of questions you could ask when you are building a network?
4. What key words would you scan bulletin boards for when you are looking for a job?
5. What headings would you look under to find government employment agencies?
6. How would you find private employment agencies in the yellow pages?
7. A "Want Ad" says "F/t worker needed, temp. 4 wks. No exp. req., just refs." What does this mean?
8. What are two reasons to use a "Work Wanted" ad?

## Critical Thinking

In Chapter 6, you listed pros and cons for buying products or services. How could you use pros and cons to help you choose a job? Write your answers on a separate sheet of paper.

## Group Activity

Work with a small group to write a short story about someone looking for a job. Your story should explain three different ways that the main character looked for a job. Include dialogue between characters and the text of ads that the main character might have read or written. Your story should end when the main character finds a job.

*Employers are impressed when job candidates fill out applications neatly and thoroughly. It is a good idea to proofread your application before you turn it in. Make sure you have filled in all the blanks.*

# Chapter 8 Applying for a Job

## Words to Know

| | |
|---|---|
| **résumé** | a written statement of a person's work experience, education, and personal information |
| **application** | a form that employers ask job-seekers to fill out with information about themselves |
| **action verbs** | words that show action, like *cook* and *run* |
| **duty** | a task performed on a job |
| **accomplishments** | things done well |
| **proofread** | to check writing carefully for mistakes |
| **cover letter** | a short letter to an employer included with a job application or résumé |

### "Help Wanted" Project

Look through the "Help Wanted" section of a newspaper. Find a job that you would like to have. Write a cover letter to send to the company to go along with your résumé.

### Learning Objectives

- Write and edit a résumé.
- Identify three techniques for filling out applications.
- Write a cover letter.

## SKILL 8.1 Write a Résumé

A **résumé** is a written statement about your background. It includes personal information, it outlines your education, and it lists your work experience and job skills. Sometimes, you can submit a résumé electronically, using e-mail.

To an employer, your résumé or job **application** represents you. For this reason, your résumé should be neat and well-written. There are many different ways to put a résumé together. The example that follows shows the parts of a résumé.

Your name
Address
Phone number

**Max Lee**
1573 Jackson Street, Apartment 12
Reno, NV 89517
(775) 555-1263

The job you want

**Objective:** Position as a computer salesperson in a retail electronics or computer store

Paid or volunteer work experience. Include dates and duties.

**Work Experience:**

6/98–6/00 Sandwich Maker. Sam's Sandwiches, 1484 Leo Drive, Reno, NV 89511. Made 100 sandwiches per eight-hour shift. Served customers, handled money.

5/97–5/98 Garden Helper. Mowed lawns, pruned trees, put in plants.

Your schooling to date

**Education:** Graduated Monroe High School, 2000
Currently enrolled in Reno Community College, majoring in Computer Science.

Any skills that might help you get the job.

**Skills:** Can operate personal computers and use 15 software packages.

People who will tell the employer about your character and work abilities.

**References:** Available upon request.

If you use a computer to write your résumé, you can easily add updates to it later.

## Practice

On a separate sheet of paper, write a first draft of your résumé. The first draft is just for getting information down on paper. Follow the model on page 98. If you do not have any paid work experience, think of work you have done at home or at school. You may have skills in child care, car repair, or yard work, for example.

## SKILL 8.2 Use Action Verbs

Once you have a first draft, you can edit your résumé. The most important part of your résumé tells about your work experience. Here, you want to use **action verbs** to describe your skills and **duties,** or tasks. Action verbs are verbs that describe doing. *Run, jump,* and *crash* are action verbs. Action verbs give life and interest to your résumé. They let you say a lot in a short space. Here are some examples of how Max Lee edited his résumé to include action verbs.

**Brush Up on the Basics**

Do you remember what a verb is? A verb is a word that expresses action or being. (See Grammar 17 in the Reference Guide.)

| **First draft** | **Second draft** |
|---|---|
| I was a sandwich maker. | Made sandwiches. |
| I was a waiter. | Served customers. |
| I also had to take money from customers. | Handled money. |
| Sometimes I had to order supplies. | Ordered supplies. |

## Everyday English

Can you think of a job where you would not need a résumé or job application?

## Practice

Edit these sentences. Make them short and to the point by using action verbs. (Hint: Cut out verbs like *was, had, did, is,* and *were*. They do not show action. Think of action verbs to replace them.)

1. I was a babysitter for three children.
2. I did the ordering of food for the restaurant.
3. I had to call people on the phone about making their appointments.

## SKILL 8.3 Edit Your Résumé

Can a résumé show how hard you work? Can it show how skilled you are? Max Lee tried to do this when he wrote "Made 100 sandwiches per eight-hour shift." This sentence helps employers know how much work Max can do in a day. It helps employers measure Max's skills.

When you edit your résumé, use numbers to help measure your skills. "Cared for children," "Cared for four children," and "Cared for 30 children," all give employers different pictures. You can also list any awards or honors you have received. If you were top employee of the month, put it on your résumé. This is a way to show your **accomplishments**, or things you have done well.

## Practice

Read the sentence pairs below. Choose the sentence that best measures a person's skills or duties. Write it on a separate sheet of paper.

1. a. Answered phone.

   b. Answered six phone lines in office; averaged three calls per minute.

2. a. Was an excellent employee.

   b. Won "Employee of the Month" award four times in one year.

3. a. Ran a four-person crew.

   b. Ran a crew.

## SKILL 8.4 Proofread Your Résumé

It is important to double-check the dates on your résumé. You need to **proofread** it, or check your writing carefully for mistakes. Use a dictionary to check the spelling. Finally, have the résumé neatly typed or printed out from a computer. If you cannot type or do not have a computer, there are services that will do this for you. A careless résumé that is full of mistakes will only turn an employer off.

**English Tip**
A good résumé should be no more than one page long when typed.

## Practice

1. Use a dictionary to check the spelling of the words in the following part of a résumé. Write the corrected part of this résumé on a separate sheet of paper.

   **Work Experience:**

   Short-order cook. Prepared and cookd an average of 60 meels per day. Supervized 4 waiters.

(Practice continues on next page.)

*(Practice continued.)*

**2.** Write the second draft of your own résumé. Use action words and numbers. Be sure to check your spelling. Print it as neatly as you can on a separate sheet of paper.

## SKILL 8.5 Fill Out Job Applications

**English and Technology**

Many large companies have company Web sites that tell you about job openings. Some companies even let you fill out an application online.

Many times, employers will ask you to fill out a job application. The application is a form similar to a résumé. All you need to do is fill in the blanks. Here are some tips for filling out job applications.

1. Read over the application before you begin. Know exactly what you will be asked to include. Check to see if the application should be typed or printed.

2. Ask the employer if you can take the application home. At home, you can check spelling and take your time.

3. Ask for two applications in case you make a mistake. What if you have only one application? Make a copy of it, or practice filling in the information on another sheet of paper. When you are happy with it, copy it onto the application.

4. Keep your résumé handy. Many times, you can simply copy information from your résumé onto your application.

5. Proofread your application before you turn it in. Check spelling and dates one more time. Make sure you have filled in all the lines. See that all boxes are checked.

Look at the job application below.

Nannetti Printing
49 Townsend Street
Alachuan, FL 32616
(904) 555-3402

N P

## Application for Employment

Name *(last)* ______________ *(first)* ______________________________

Address ____________________________________________________

______________________________ Home phone (____) __________

Social Security Number ______________ Date of birth ______________

Position desired __________________ Date you can start __________

Are you employed now? ______________________________________

If so, may we speak to your present employer? __________________

**Education**

Circle last year completed. Descibe any other training or education.

Middle School 6 7 8 ______________________________

High School 1 2 3 4 ______________________________

College 1 2 3 4 ______________________________

**Work History**

| Name of company | Dates Worked | Position |
|---|---|---|
| | | |
| | | |
| | | |

Computer Skills: ______________________________________________

______________________________________________________________

**References**

| Name | Phone Number |
|---|---|
| 1. | (____) |
| 2. | (____) |
| 3. | (____) |

What information could you copy from your résumé onto this job application?

## Practice

Write three tips for filling out a job application. Use a separate sheet of paper.

### Your Social Security Number

Most job applications ask for your social security number. If you do not have a social security number, call your nearest Social Security Office. The people there will give you directions on how to get one. How do you find the Social Security Office? Look in the white pages of your phone book under the heading "United States Government." Then look under the subheading "Health and Human Services."

## SKILL 8.6 Write a Cover Letter

It is a good idea to include a **cover letter** with your résumé or job application. The cover letter is a way to make your résumé more personal. A cover letter might include

- the job title you are applying for.
- special skills not included on your résumé.
- reasons why you want to work for that company.

Cover letters should always be short and to the point. Look at the example of a cover letter on the next page.

### English and Careers

For a large company, you will often direct your letter to the Human Resources department. "Dear Human Resources Officer:" and "Greetings:" are appropriate ways to begin your letter. The greeting "Dear Madam or Sir:" is also acceptable.

1622 University Avenue
Davis, CA 95616

April 7, 2000

Richard S. Garcia, D.M.V.
91 Walnut Street
Davis, CA 95616

Dear Dr. Garcia:

Do you have an opening for a veterinary assistant? If you do, I would like to apply for the position.

I will be graduating from high school in June, and I will then be available for full-time work. I grew up on a farm and have had experience raising and caring for farm animals and pets. Because I love animals, I would like to learn more about caring for them.

I have included my résumé.

Sincerely,

*Carl Thomas*

Carl Thomas

## Practice

Write a cover letter to the Human Resources Department, Chicken and Chips, 1245 F Street, Boston, MA 34783. In the letter, ask if there are any management openings in your area. Mention that you are enclosing your résumé. In your cover letter, include anything else you think is important.

Chapter

# 8 Review

## Summary


Résumés and job applications help you get a job. They should be well-written and neat.

A résumé usually has these parts: personal information, education, work experience, and skills.

The purpose of the first draft of the résumé is to get information on paper. The second draft should include action verbs and words to measure your skills.

Check spelling and dates on résumés and job applications.

The cover letter is short and to the point. It tells the reason you are writing.


| |
|---|
| résumé |
| accomplishment |
| action verbs |
| proofread |
| duty |
| application |
| cover letter |

## Vocabulary Review

**Complete each sentence with a term from the box. Use a separate sheet of paper.**

1. A ____ is often sent in with job applications and résumés.
2. A task performed on a job is a ____.
3. A thing done well is an ____.
4. A ____ is a written report of your work experience and skills.
5. To check writing carefully for mistakes is to ____.
6. Employers often ask job-seekers to fill out an ____ with information about themselves.
7. Words such as *cook* and *run* are ____.

## Chapter Quiz

**Answer the following questions in one or two sentences. Use a separate sheet of paper.**

1. What is a résumé? Why should it be neat?
2. What is the difference between a first draft and a second draft?
3. What are the key parts of a résumé?
4. How can action words make a résumé stronger?
5. How can you add action to this sentence? *I was the football coach's helper.*
6. How do numbers or measurements in a résumé make your skills seem stronger?
7. How can you edit this item so that it includes a measurement? *Sewed clothes for school fashion show.*
8. Why is it a good idea to take a résumé with you when you plan to fill out a job application?
9. What three things should a cover letter include?

## Critical Thinking

Juan wants to consult a "How-To" book on writing résumés. How would he find it in a library? Write your answer on a separate sheet of paper.

## Group Activity

Interview a partner about his or her work experience, duties, skills, and goals. Take notes and write the information in résumé form. Write a first draft and a second draft. Your second draft should include action words and words for measuring skills. Return the draft to your partner to see whether it is correct.

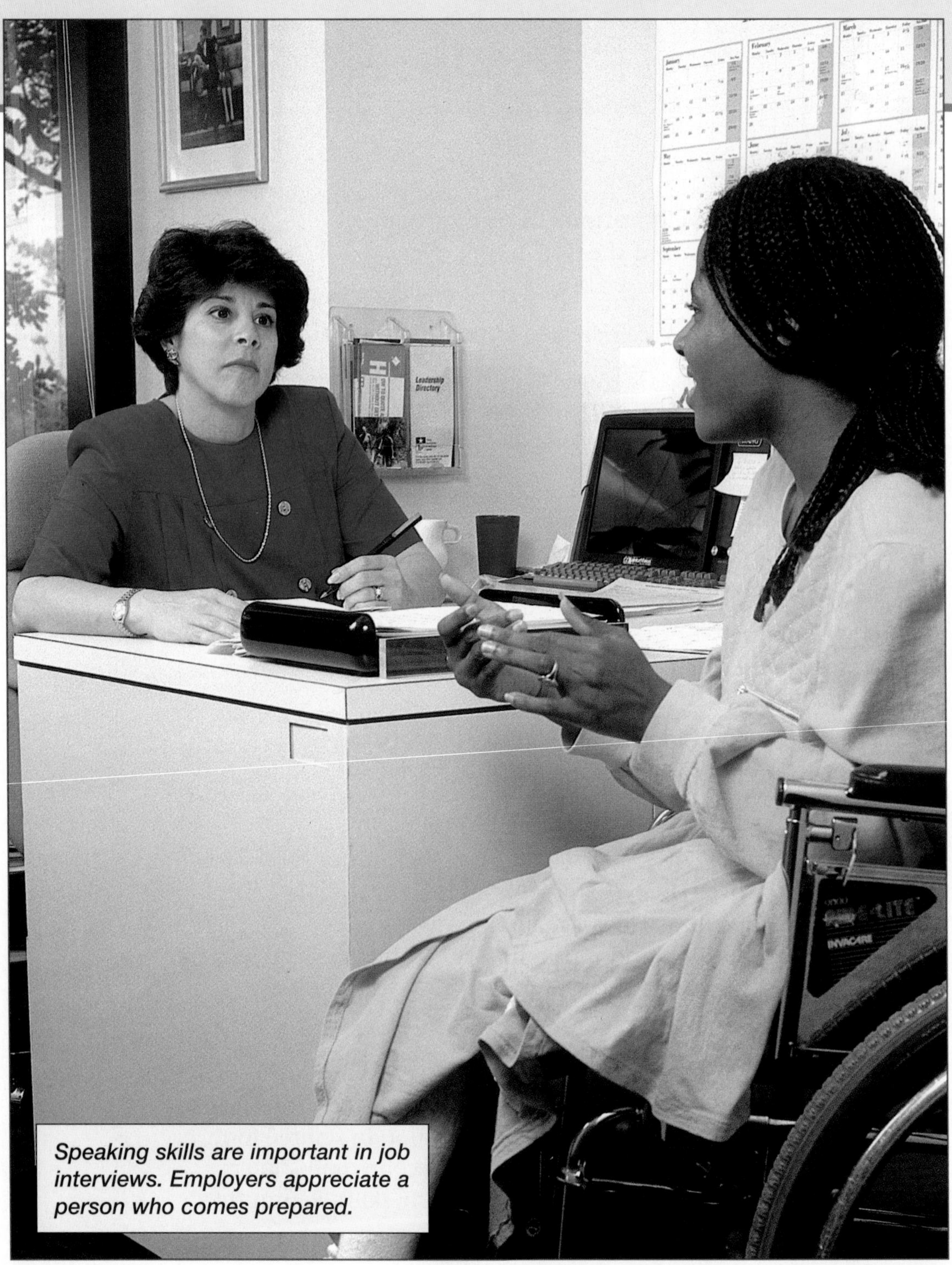


*Speaking skills are important in job interviews. Employers appreciate a person who comes prepared.*

# Chapter 9 Interviewing

## Words to Know

| | |
|---|---|
| **co-workers** | people you work with |
| **confident** | sure of yourself |
| **slang** | an informal language that is not considered part of correct English |
| **role model** | a person you want to be like and learn from |
| **pronounce** | to say a word out loud |
| **body language** | messages given by the body |
| **visualization** | picturing something |

## Job Interview Project

Work with a partner to role-play a job interview. One partner takes the role of the interviewer, while the other partner takes the role of the person being interviewed. Switch roles. Then, write a follow-up letter to restate your interest in the job.

## Learning Objectives

- Prepare questions and answers for interviews.
- Identify and practice methods for speaking clearly.
- Identify and practice good body language for interviews.
- Write a follow-up letter.

## SKILL 9.1 Prepare for Interviews

You are interviewing a person for a job. You ask a question. The person looks surprised, and then starts to answer. "Uh, uh, well, I don't know," the person says.

**English and Careers**

Employers often begin an interview with, *Tell me about yourself.* How would you prepare to answer this question?

Employers are often looking for people who are prepared to talk about themselves. Some questions that employers ask are easy to prepare for. For example,

- Will you take part-time work?
- Do you have experience in this field?
- How will you get to work every day?

Other questions require more thought. You should be ready to answer them. Before you go to an interview, ask yourself these five questions. Then write the answers on a separate sheet of paper.

1. Why do you want to work here?

Employers want someone who will be part of the team. They want someone who *wants* to work for them. To prepare, you might ask other workers what they like about the company. You might tell the employer what you think it would be like to work there.

2. What are your strengths?

Before the interview, write down three of your strengths. Think of your skills and the things people like about you. Be honest about yourself. Don't be shy, and don't brag. If you are skilled at typing, say so. If people like working with you, let the interviewer know that.

3. What are your weaknesses?

Think of three weaknesses that can also be strengths. For example, you may be easily bothered by lazy **co-workers,** or people you work with. This could mean you are a hard worker yourself. A weakness could also be something you have not learned yet. You can simply tell the employer you are ready and willing to learn. Employers can think of this weakness as a strength.

4. Why should we hire you instead of someone else?

Restate your skills and your willingness to work. Employers want to know that you are **confident,** or sure of yourself.

5. Why did you leave your other jobs?

You should be honest and positive. Perhaps you wanted more money, or you did not like the work. If you were fired, explain why. Never speak badly about your former employers.

## Practice

Complete the following activities on a separate sheet of paper.

**1.** Think of a company you would like to work for. List three reasons that the company appeals to you.

**2.** List three of your strengths and three of your weaknesses. Use weaknesses that can also be seen as strengths.

**3.** You were fired from your last job. You did not get along with your boss. Write down how you will answer the question: *Why did you leave your last job?*

## SKILL 9.2 Pronounce Words Clearly

**Everyday English**

Synonyms are words with similar meanings. What are synonyms for some slang words?

Turn on the radio or television. Listen to the news announcer speaking. Can you understand every word? Does the person sound relaxed? Do you hear **slang,** or informal language? Slang is not considered part of standard, or correct, English.

A news announcer is a good **role model,** or person you want to be like, for clear speech. In an interview, you should **pronounce,** or say out loud, every word clearly. Speak loudly enough to be heard—but not so loudly that you are shouting. You want to sound sincere and pleasant. Do not be overly friendly, either. Remember, you are there on business.

You can do several things to improve your speech.

- Practice your interview answers in front of a mirror. Watch your mouth as you pronounce each word. Use your facial muscles and lips to say words clearly.
- Take a deep breath before you speak. This will relax you and give strength to your voice.
- Speak into a tape recorder. Play it back and listen to yourself. What sounds good? How can you improve?
- Act out the interview with a friend. Do it a few times so you get to the point where you do not need your notes. Listen to the comments your friend makes about your speech, and then work to improve it.

### Practice

Complete the following activities.

**1.** Feel your face muscles, lips, and tongue move as you say these words: *I am going to Iowa to practice my speech.*

2. Have a classmate act as the job interviewer. Tell him or her about your strengths.

3. Ask your classmate for feedback on these things.
   - How clearly you express your points
   - How strong your voice is
   - How relaxed you sound

4. On a separate sheet of paper, write two things you do well. Write two things you need to improve.

### A Word About Slang

Interviewers like to hear correct grammar without slang. Which sentence is better for an interview: *I ain't that kind of dude* or *I am not that kind of person*?

## SKILL 9.3 Use Body Language Effectively

Sandy thought she was all prepared for an interview. She had practiced speaking. Her voice and words were clear and true, but during the interview, she stared at the employer's desk. It really did not matter what she said. Her eyes said that she was scared.

Using the right **body language**, or messages sent by the body, is so important that it is actually considered a speaking skill. Here are some "do's" and "don'ts" for body language.

- Do make eye contact. Don't stare.
- Do smile occasionally. Don't grin or frown.
- Do nod your head up and down thoughtfully. Don't look away.
- Do keep your chin up.

### English and Careers

Many employers look for job applicants with clear, strong voices. Do you speak clearly? Is that a skill you need to practice?

- Do use your hands in an open, friendly way. Don't point, cross your arms, or wring your hands together.
- Do sit tall. Don't slouch.
- Do keep your feet on the floor and your legs together. Don't shake your feet.

## Practice

List the "do's" of body language on a separate sheet of paper. Then practice one of your interview questions in front of a mirror. Check to make sure you are following each of the "do's."

### See It in Your Head

Before a big tennis match, some players picture the game. In their minds they "see" their perfect strokes. They return serves with power. They win the game.

Seeing success in your mind is called **visualization**, or picturing something. Visualization can help you be more confident. It is a simple, quiet way to prepare. To visualize, just close your eyes. Take a deep breath. See your relaxed smile. Hear your clear voice. Be impressed by your great answers. At the real interview, those English skills you visualized will be easier to act out.

## SKILL 9.4 Write a Follow-Up Letter

What do you do when you have completed the interview process? First, it is a good idea to write a follow-up letter to the person who interviewed you.

In this letter, you should restate your interest in the job. You should also thank the person for the time he or she took to interview you. Be sure to spell the interviewer's name and the company's name correctly. Also, be sure that you write the address of the company or store correctly.

**Brush Up on the Basics**

Remember to use a colon (:) after the greeting in a business letter. (See Punctuation 21 in the Reference Guide.)

Study this example.

463 Oak Avenue
San Pedro, CA 90733

July 18, 2000

Paulette Davis
Personnel Director
Tiny Tot Day Care Center
1982 Parker Drive
San Mateo, CA 94403

Dear Ms. Davis:

Thank you for the time you spent interviewing me on July 17. I would like to tell you again how interested I am in working for Tiny Tot Day Care Center. I believe that my experience in the field of child care qualifies me for the position that is open.

Very truly yours,
*Sharon Martin*
Sharon Martin

## Practice

On a separate sheet of paper, write a follow-up letter. Use correct business letter form. Follow the style of the example above.

Chapter

# 9 Review

## Summary

| |
|---|
| Speaking skills are important in job interviews. Interviewers like people who come prepared. |
| To prepare for an interview, it is a good idea to write down the answers to questions that might be asked. |
| Interviewers like clear, strong speech. |
| Body language is just as important as what you say. Sit tall, keep your chin up, and make eye contact. |
| It is important to write a follow-up letter after an interview. |

| |
|---|
| co-workers |
| confident |
| pronounce |
| slang |
| body language |
| role model |
| visualization |

## Vocabulary Review

**Match each term in the box with its meaning. Write the term and its matching number on a separate sheet of paper.**

1. messages given by the body
2. informal language
3. sure of yourself
4. people you work with
5. to say a word out loud
6. picturing something
7. a person you want to be like

## Chapter Quiz

**Answer the following questions in one or two sentences. Use a separate sheet of paper.**

1. Why is it important to prepare for an interview?
2. What are the five questions you should prepare for?
3. What is an example of a weakness that could be seen as a strength? Explain.
4. When asked why he left his last job, Julio said, "I couldn't stand that place. It was dirty. There were bugs everywhere." What did he do wrong?
5. What is a better answer that Julio could have given?
6. How should your voice and words sound when you speak at an interview?
7. What is one good way to practice speaking?
8. What are two "do's" and two "don'ts" for body language?
9. How can visualization help you prepare for an interview?

## Critical Thinking

Write down four questions you might ask in a job interview. For example: *If I do my job well, what kind of future do I have here?*

## Group Activity

Work with a small group to list five things you might tell a friend who is nervous about a job interview. What advice can you give him or her? Then exchange lists with another group. Suggest ways that the group might improve its list.

*After finishing the paperwork, it is time to start learning your new job duties. A senior employee usually shows you around and shows you how things are done.*

# Chapter 10 Beginning Work

## Words to Know

| | |
|---|---|
| **policies** | the rules of a company |
| **benefits** | extras, such as health insurance, for workers |
| **human resources department** | a company department that hires employees and helps them solve problems |
| **acronym** | an abbreviation based on the first letters of words in a title or slogan |
| **Statement of Earnings and Deductions** | the part of a paycheck stub telling how much money was earned and how much was deducted |
| **deductions** | money taken from a paycheck for taxes and other things |

### Employee Handbook Project

You own a clothing store. Write a table of contents for an employee handbook that you will give to people who work in the store. You may want to go to a clothing store and take notes on what you think should be included in the employee handbook.

### Learning Objectives

- Describe three kinds of information found in employee handbooks.
- Use the table of contents to see what is covered in an employee handbook.
- Identify two ways the index and glossary of an employee handbook can be used.
- Explain two tips for filling out forms.
- Identify three key words found on paycheck stubs.

## SKILL 10.1 Study the Employee Handbook

Most companies have employee handbooks. Many times, these books look big and unfriendly, but they can give you important information about the company you are working for. Most often, they contain information about the following things.

- **The company's policies.** A company's rules, or **policies**, are the "do's" and "don'ts" you need to know. Companies often have policies about what you should wear to work. They have policies about being late and taking breaks. They might even have a policy about having food at your desk. Knowing the policies can help save you from embarrassing moments. These policies can help you become comfortable on the job.

- **Worker benefits.** Most companies offer some kind of **benefits**, or extras, to their workers. The employee handbook often explains these benefits to you. For example, your company may offer you a choice of health plans. The employee handbook usually tells what the plans are and how to sign up for them.

- **The company departments and what they do.** A large company usually has many departments. Knowing these departments and what they do can make your life simpler. For example, suppose you have questions about health plans. You could look in the employee handbook to see if the company has a **human resources department.** The people there help workers with questions about overtime or missed paychecks. They can also answer health plan questions and tell you what to do about other common problems.

## Practice

Tomorrow is Halloween, so you are thinking about dressing up like a clown and going to work. Can the employee handbook help you decide if this is a good idea? Explain your answer on a separate sheet of paper.

## SKILL 10.2 Use the Employee Handbook

Employee handbooks are sometimes very large books. Knowing where and how to find the information you need is very important. The table of contents can help you. First, look over the table of contents. Read the chapters that are most important to you first. Take notes to remember key information. You can wait until later to read sections of the handbook that are less important to you.

**English and Careers**

When would be a good time for you to study the employee handbook?

## Practice

Complete the following activity on a separate sheet of paper.

It is your first day on the job. You open up your employee handbook. This is the table of contents.

**Table of Contents**

I. Your First Day on the Job
II. Choosing a Health Plan
III. History of the Company
IV. Opportunities
V. Your Work Review
VI. Sick Leave and Holidays
VII. All About Pay

*(Practice continues on next page.)* ⇨

*(Practice continued.)*

**English Tip**
What if you left your handbook at home? If you need a quick answer, you can always ask a co-worker to help you.

Remember, it is your first day on the job. You have been told that you do not have to sign up for a health plan for ninety days. You also have been told that you will have your first work review after the first ninety days.

Read the sections of the table of contents. Put them in the order in which they are important to you. Explain why you put them in that order.

### Finding Key Information

You work at a fast food restaurant. This restaurant has rules for everything. Before your first shift, you want to quickly review how to greet customers.

Remember, you can find this kind of information quickly by using the index. Simply look up "greeting customers" in the back of the book. You will probably find an entry.

### Special Words on the Job

It is your third week on the job. Your boss comes up to you and says, "Fill out a STAR report." Then she or he disappears. You do not know what a STAR report is. How can you find out?

You will often have to learn special words for doing your job. When you need help with these words, look in the glossary or index of your employee handbook. STAR is probably an **acronym**, or an abbreviation based on first letters of words in a title or slogan. For example, STAR could stand for South Texas Account Report. By using the employee handbook, you can find out what STAR is and how to fill out a STAR report.

## Practice

Answer the following questions about the employee handbook on a separate sheet of paper.

1. What are three reasons to read the employee handbook?

2. Your boss tells you to talk to the PPO. Where would you find what PPO stands for?

3. You want to know if the company offers life insurance. To find out, where in the index would you look?

## SKILL 10.3 Fill Out Forms

Today's work world is filled with papers, reports, and computers. During your first week on the job, you will probably have to fill out a few forms. These forms help a company keep track of who you are and what you should be paid. For example, look at the W-4 form on page 124. This form helps your employer know how much in taxes to keep out of your paycheck.

**Brush Up on the Basics**

The names of people, streets, cities, and states should begin with a capital letter. (See Capitalization 3 and 9–11 in the Reference Guide.)

At a first look, the W-4 is confusing. Here are some English skills to help you fill out the W-4 and other forms like it.

- Read the entire form before you fill it out.
- Make a list of words or directions that you do not understand.

- Go to your supervisor or the human resources department where you work. Get the answers to your questions before you start filling out the forms. Do not feel embarrassed about asking questions. You are new on the job. Asking questions is a sign that you are willing and able to learn.
- Fill out the form neatly.
- Have your supervisor or the human resources department check it over.
- Turn in the form on time.

- - - - - - - - - - - - - - - Cut here and give form W-4 to your employer. Keep the top part for your records. - - - - - - - - - - - - - - -

Form **W-4**
Department of the Treasury
Internal Revenue Service

**Employee's Withholding Allowance Certificate**

▶ **For Privacy Act and Paperwork Reduction Act Notice, see page 2.**

**2001**

1 Type or print your first name and middle initial | Last name | **2** Your Social Security number

Home address (number and street or rural route)

**3** ☐ Single ☐ Married ☐ Married, but withhold at higher Single rate.
**Note:** *If married, but legally separated, or spouse is a nonresident alien, check the Single box.*

City or town, state, and ZIP code

**4** If your last name differs from that on your Social Security card, check here. **You must call 1-800-772-1213 for a new card** . . . ▶ ☐

**5** Total number of allowances you are claiming (from line H above or from the worksheets on page 2 if they apply) . | 5 |

**6** Additional amount, if any, you want withheld from each paycheck . . . . . . . . . . . . . . . . . | 6 | $

**7** I claim exemption from withholding for 2001, and I certify that I meet **BOTH** of the following conditions for exemption:
- Last year I had a right to a refund of **ALL** Federal income tax withheld because I had **NO** tax liability; **AND**
- This year I expect a refund of **ALL** Federal income tax withheld because I expect to have **NO** tax liability.

If you meet both conditions, write EXEMPT here . . . . . . ▶ | 7 |

Under penalties of perjury, I certify that I am entitled to the number of withholding allowances claimed on this certificate, or I am entitled to claim exempt status.
**Employee's signature**
(Form is not valid unless you sign it) ▶ **Date** ▶

**8** Employer's name and address (Employer: Complete 8 and 10 only if sending to the IRS.) | **9** Office code (optional) | **10** Employer identification number

## Practice

Complete the following activities on a separate sheet of paper.

1. Look at the W-4 form, "Employee's Withholding Allowance Certificate" on page 124. You are going to fill it out. Make a list of the words you do not know.

2. Look over the directions. Write down any questions you have about filling out the form.

3. Who would you ask to find out the answers to your questions?

## SKILL 10.4 Interpret Your Paycheck Stub

Finally, payday comes. You are handed a paycheck. Attached to it is your paycheck stub. This is called a **Statement of Earnings and Deductions.** You need to read the paycheck stub carefully to make sure you are getting the right amount of money. The stub shows the following things.

- How much money you earned (gross pay)
- What **deductions**, or money taken from a paycheck for taxes and other things, were taken from your earned pay
- Your take-home pay (net pay)

At first, you might be confused by so much information. Here is how to make sense of a paycheck stub.

1. Look at each box or section as one piece of information.
2. Read each piece of information carefully.
3. Make a list of questions.
4. Go to a co-worker, your supervisor, or the human resources department to get your questions answered.

Look at the sample paycheck stub below.

**CORVALIS SHIPPING CENTER** LENOX MILL, OH

| EMPLOYEE NUMBER | CURRENT HOURS | | | YEAR TO DATE | | | | | |
|---|---|---|---|---|---|---|---|---|---|
| | PAY RATE/HR | REGULAR | OVERTIME | Y.T.D. GROSS | F.I.T. | F.I.C.A. | LOCAL | STATE | RET. |
| 017338 | 6 00 | 29 50 | 00 | 1115 25 | 71 70 | 65 24 | 11 16 | 22 31 | 9 29 |

| CURRENT EARNINGS | | | CURRENT | | | | | |
|---|---|---|---|---|---|---|---|---|
| REGULAR | OVERTIME | SPECIAL | CURRENT GROSS | F.I.T. | F.I.C.A. | LOCAL | STATE | RET. |
| 177 00 | 00 | 00 | 177 00 | 13 77 | 10 35 | 1 77 | 3 54 | 9 29 |

| CHECK NO. | DESCRIPTION | AMOUNT | DESCRIPTION | AMOUNT | TOTAL DEDUCTIONS |
|---|---|---|---|---|---|
| 046790 | | | | | 38 72 |

| ENDING DATE |
|---|
| 09 03 00 |

| CHECK DATE |
|---|
| 09 03 00 |

AUTHORIZED DEDUCTIONS AND SPECIAL PAY ELEMENTS

| NET PAY |
|---|
| 138 28 |

STATEMENT OF EARNINGS AND DEDUCTIONS • DETACH AND RETAIN FOR YOUR RECORDS

### Vocabulary for Reading Your Paycheck Stub

Your paycheck stub has many new words. Look at the list of words, abbreviations, and their meanings on the top of the next page.

| | |
|---|---|
| **Ending Date** | The last day of the pay period |
| **Current Gross** | The total amount of money you earned in the pay period |
| **Y.T.D.** | Year-to-date |
| **Net pay** | The amount of money you earned after all deductions were made. This is your take-home pay. It is the actual amount of money your check is worth. |
| **F.I.T.** | Federal income tax |
| **F.I.C.A.** | Social security tax; the letters stand for Federal Insurance Contribution Act |
| **Local** | Local taxes, such as county or city tax |
| **State** | State taxes |
| **Ret.** | Retirement fund |
| **Regular** | Hours or pay at your usual rate |
| **Overtime** | Hours or pay over your usual rate |

**Everyday English**

How can understanding your paycheck stub help you plan your work schedule? How can it help you plan your budget?

## Practice

Use the vocabulary list above to answer these questions about the paycheck stub on page 126.

**1.** How much social security tax was taken out of this employee's pay?

**2.** Did this employee work any overtime hours?

**3.** What is this employee's gross pay for the pay period?

**4.** How much gross pay has this employee earned this year?

**5.** What is this employee's net pay?

Chapter

# 10 Review

## Summary

| Most employee handbooks contain information about worker benefits and company policies. |
|---|
| Look over the chapters in your employee handbook to find the information that is most important to you. |
| Use the index and glossary of the employee handbook to find key information and learn special words. |
| To fill out forms carefully, read through them first. Make notes about words and directions before you fill out the forms. Ask co-workers, supervisors, or the human resources department for help. |
| Read paycheck stubs carefully. Look at each piece of information and learn what it means. |

| human resources department |
|---|
| acronym |
| benefits |
| policies |
| deductions |
| Statement of Earnings and Deductions |

## Vocabulary Review

**Match each term in the box with its meaning. Write the term and its matching number on a separate sheet of paper.**

1. extras, such as health insurance, for workers
2. a company's rules
3. money taken from a paycheck for taxes and other things
4. a company department that hires employees and helps them solve problems
5. the part of a paycheck telling how much money was earned and how much was deducted
6. an abbreviation based on the first letters of words in a title or slogan

## Chapter Quiz

**Answer the following questions in one or two sentences. Use a separate sheet of paper.**

1. What are three things usually found in an employee handbook?
2. What is the first thing you should do with an employee handbook?
3. What is one example of how you might use the index of an employee handbook?
4. Your boss tells you to check with the RRD. How could you use an employee handbook to help you find out what the RRD is?
5. Why might you take notes when you read an employee handbook?
6. What is a common form you will fill out at work?
7. If a form confuses you, what should you do?
8. Why is it important to read the Statement of Earnings and Deductions?
9. How are gross pay and net pay different?

## Critical Thinking

Do you think a dictionary could help you read a paycheck stub? Explain your answer.

## Group Activity

Work with a group to write a scene about someone's first day at work. The characters are an employee and his or her boss. The boss is too busy to train the new employee. The employee does not know how to work the copier machine. What should he or she do? What is the outcome of his or her decision?

Learning difficult job skills takes hard work and patience. It helps to use job aids like charts and step-by-step instructions.

# Chapter 11 Learning Job Skills

## Words to Know

| | |
|---|---|
| **job aid** | anything that helps people do their job correctly |
| **procedure** | the steps you follow to accomplish a task |
| **task** | a small part of a large job |

### Job Aid Project

You have just gotten a job as a cashier at a fast food restaurant. Create a job aid that will help you perform one aspect of your job, such as how to treat customers or how to work a cash register.

### Learning Objectives

- Describe what a job aid is.
- Identify the steps in using different job aids.
- Name three common types of job aids.
- Write or make a job aid.

## SKILL 11.1 Use Job Aids

A **job aid** is anything that helps you learn or do your job correctly. Job aids can be forms, lists of steps, instructions, manuals, and so on. Here are three examples of common job aids and how to use them.

**Brush Up on the Basics**

Remember to use a colon (:) between the hour and the minutes when you write the time. (See Punctuation 22 in the Reference Guide.)

### A Telephone Message Form

This job aid tells you the key information to get from a person when you are taking a message. A sample telephone job aid is show below.

**MESSAGE** Date ______ Time ______

For ____________________

From ____________________

Of ____________________

Phone Number ____________________

| | |
|---|---|
| ☐ Telephoned | ☐ Please call |
| ☐ Came to see you | ☐ Will call again |
| ☐ Wants to see you | ☐ Returned your call |

Message ____________________

____________________

____________________

____________________

____________________

Taken by ____________________

To use this job aid, keep it in front of you when you answer the phone. Get the key information you need from the caller, such as his or her name, phone number, where the caller is from, and the message. Fill in the rest of the information, such as the date, time, and your name, as soon as you hang up. This saves you and the caller time on the phone.

### A Work Schedule

In some types of jobs, your hours may change from week to week. In such cases, work schedules are posted to let you know your weekly shifts. Often, these job aids are in chart form. To read them, simply use your skills from Chapter 2. Here is an example of a work schedule.

| | M | T | W | Th | F |
|---|---|---|---|---|---|
| Abrams, J. | 8 A.M. to 1 P.M. | 8 A.M. to 1 P.M. | 12 noon to 5 P.M. | 8 A.M. to 1 P.M. | 12 noon to 5 P.M. |
| Liu, M. | 12 noon to 5 P.M. | 12 noon to 5 P.M. | 8 A.M. to 1 P.M. | 4 P.M. to 8 P.M. | 4 P.M. to 8 P.M. |
| Scott, C. | 6 P.M. to 10 P.M. | 6 P.M. to 10 P.M. | 6 P.M. to 10 P.M. | 12 noon to 5 P.M. | 8 A.M. to 1 P.M. |

### A "How-To" Job Aid

A "How-To" job aid is a list of step-by-step instructions. Perhaps it tells you an office **procedure**, or the steps you follow to accomplish a task. Usually, these instructions are written out. Here is an example of a "How-To" job aid found in a small business office.

**Everyday English**

What are some job aids you use to operate machines in your home?

Closing Procedures

1. Check to see that all computers and typewriters are off.
2. Turn on answering machine.
3. Close drapes.
4. Turn on alarm.
5. Shut off lights.
6. Lock the door.

**English and Technology**

You can use a word processing program to create a file for the job aid information you need.

These job aids are usually simple to follow. You just have to read them and carry out the steps one by one.

## Practice

Use a separate sheet of paper to answer these questions.

1. What might happen if you waited to fill out the telephone message form until after you hung up the phone?
2. Look at the work schedule on page 133. What hours does M. Liu work on Wednesday?
3. You want to work an evening shift on Monday. Who would you ask to switch with you?

## SKILL 11.2 Make Your Own Job Aid

Jerry has the new responsibility of opening up the restaurant where he works each morning. His boss did not give him a job aid for opening up the restaurant. Jerry decided to make one for himself. Here is his job aid.

*Opening*

*1. Put in alarm key and turn.*

*2. Punch code X12238.*

*Alarm Company: 555-9000*

*My code: 990002*

Jerry kept this job aid in his wallet. That way, no one else could see the secret codes.

Many times when you are learning job skills, people will tell you how to do something. It can be hard to remember all the steps after hearing them just once. To make your own job aid, you should

1. listen carefully for each step of the way to perform a **task**, or small part of a large job.
2. write down the steps in order.
3. include any other important information on the job aid.
4. put the job aid in a place where it is easy to use.

**English Tip**
To make a job aid that is most effective, write down the information you need, and keep it where you can easily find it.

## Practice

Make a job aid out of these instructions.

> You are going to have to learn how to file these reports. It is really easy. Just look for the report name. You can find it on the top right of the report cover. Well, sometimes it is at the bottom. Then file the reports alphabetically. Don't forget to take out the yellow sheet in each report first. Take the yellow sheets marked "Yes" to shipping. Put the yellow sheets marked "No" in the trash can.

Chapter

# 11 Review

## Summary

| |
|---|
| A job aid is anything you can use to help you learn and remember job skills. |
| Common job aids are forms, charts, and "How-To" instructions. |
| Making a job aid is a good way to learn skills on the job. |
| Job aids should include step-by-step instructions. They should also include key information about how to do a task. |

| |
|---|
| job aid |
| task |
| procedure |

## Vocabulary Review

**Match each term in the box with its meaning. Write the term and its matching number on a separate sheet of paper.**

**1.** a small part of a large job

**2.** the steps you follow to accomplish a task

**3.** anything that helps people do their job correctly

## Chapter Quiz

**Answer the following questions in one or two sentences. Use a separate sheet of paper.**

1. What is a job aid?
2. How is a telephone message form a job aid?
3. What kinds of information do you usually take down while a caller is on the phone?
4. What kinds of information do you usually fill in after the caller has hung up?
5. Why is a work schedule considered a job aid?
6. What are "How-To" job aids?
7. What are two examples of "How-To" job aids?
8. What do "How-To" job aids usually include?
9. Why is it a good idea to carry a pad and pencil with you while you are learning a new job?
10. Why should job aids be easy to use?

## Critical Thinking

Is listening an important skill for every worker? Explain your answer.

### Group Activity

Work with a group to write a job aid for someone who has been hired to take care of a house while the owners are away on vacation. The job aid should be about one of the important tasks that need to be done, such as feeding the dog or locking up the house.

*Good customer service requires good communication skills. Who else do you have to communicate with when you are on the job?*

# Chapter 12 Communicating at Work

## Words to Know

| | |
|---|---|
| **communication** | the giving and receiving of information |
| **presentation** | the act of showing or explaining something to another person or group |
| **memo** | a short note |
| **topic sentence** | a sentence that introduces the subject or states the purpose |

## Memo-Writing Project

You have a part-time job working in an office after school. Write a list of at least four suggestions you would like to give to Mr. Jones, your boss. Use an outline to organize your suggestions. Then, write a memo to Mr. Jones telling him your suggestions.

## Learning Objectives

- Identify three ways to communicate on the job.
- Write an outline of a business message.
- Explain at least three rules for good business writing.
- Identify two ways to deal with angry customers.

## SKILL 12.1 Communicate on the Job

**Communication** is the giving and receiving of information. You communicate daily with family and friends. When communication breaks down, a misunderstanding may occur. If communication breaks down on the job, important things do not get done.

> **English and Careers**
>
> The word *memo* sounds like the word memory. Why do you think this is so?

There are many ways of communicating on the job. Suppose that you want to tell your boss about a great idea. You could make a **presentation** in person or in writing. What if you need to get important information to your co-workers? Just write a **memo.** A memo is a short note.

### The Employee Handbook and Communication

Many times, companies have formal ways, or procedures, for solving employee problems. As you learned in Chapter 10, you can look up these procedures in the employee handbook.

## Practice

Use a separate sheet of paper to answer these questions.

1. What kinds of problems do you think could be caused by poor communication on the job?
2. How could good communication improve a workplace?
3. What are two good ways to communicate on the job?

## SKILL 12.2 Use an Outline

Whether you are planning to communicate in person or in writing, you must prepare. One of the best ways to prepare is to make an outline.

Most of the time, the type of outline you will use looks like the one below.

> **English Tip**
> An outline can help you plan a memo, a presentation, and many other kinds of communication on the job.

I. **Topic sentence**
   The **topic sentence** tells the reason you are writing (or speaking).

II. **Supporting Sentences or Body**
   A.
   B.
   C.

   Supporting sentences are the facts that explain or support the topic sentence. The body contains the important information.

III. **Closing Sentences**
   In your closing sentences, you usually tell what you want the outcome of your presentation to be, or you might thank people for reading or listening to your ideas.

On the next page is an example of a filled-in outline. The writer, Jamal, is going to make his presentation in person to his boss. He is preparing his ideas on paper.

**Everyday English**

Look back at Chapter 9. Review the body language you used in interviews. Should this body language be used in all kinds of spoken communication? Explain.

I. **I want to suggest ways to improve the office.**

II. **My ideas are as follows:**

   A. Move the receptionist and phone to the far wall. This will keep the rest of the office quieter. Workers will be able to concentrate better.

   B. Move the copy machine into the back room. This will give us more room for files. It will also keep the front office quieter.

III. **Thank you for listening. I appreciate it.**

Notice Jamal's supporting sentences. He tells exactly how his suggestions will improve the office, and he does not let his feelings get in the way. Suppose he had made his presentation like this: *It is too noisy in that front office. Nobody can work. If you don't quiet it down, I'll quit and so will everybody else.* Jamal would sound angry, and his approach would be very negative.

## Practice

André is bussing tables at a busy restaurant. His co-worker is not doing his share. For four days in a row, André has had to clean tables in his co-worker's section. In addition, André has had to sweep both sections twice this week. However, they split tips down the middle. André would like his co-worker to get busy and do his share. He is angry about the situation.

On a separate sheet of paper, prepare an outline of what André might say to his co-worker.

## SKILL 12.3 Put It in Writing

Suppose Jamal's boss took his suggestions. His boss might put out an e-mail message that looks like the one on the next page.

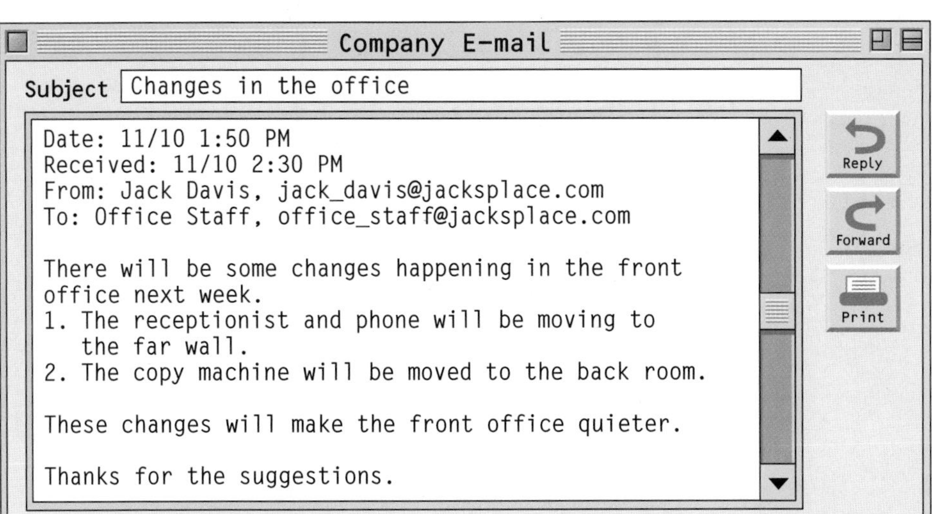
Company E-mail

Subject: Changes in the office

Date: 11/10 1:50 PM
Received: 11/10 2:30 PM
From: Jack Davis, jack_davis@jacksplace.com
To: Office Staff, office_staff@jacksplace.com

There will be some changes happening in the front office next week.
1. The receptionist and phone will be moving to the far wall.
2. The copy machine will be moved to the back room.

These changes will make the front office quieter.

Thanks for the suggestions.



The e-mail message follows rules of good business writing. The writing is to the point. The words are simple. Good business writing should save the reader's time and be understandable. Long words and sentences get in the way of the meaning.

Whenever you are writing on the job, follow the rules below.

**Rules for Writing on the Job**

1. Write an outline, a first draft, and a final draft.
2. Use a topic sentence, supporting sentences, and a closing.
3. Write your drafts in short, complete sentences.
4. Stick to the facts that matter. Do not go on and on about your feelings.
5. Always remember to check your spelling and proofread your final draft. Use a dictionary or a spell-checker.

**English and Technology**

Using e-mail is a good way to communicate on the job. You can use e-mail to send memos to your co-workers or a thank-you note to a customer.

## Practice

> **Brush Up on the Basics**
> Prepositional phrases can add detail to nouns and verbs in a report. (See Grammar 52–53 in the Reference Guide.)

Here is an accident report. Write a final draft of the report on a separate sheet of paper. Use the *Rules for Writing on the Job* on page 143.

> This is a report of the accident that happened on June 18th. It was terrible. I was standing by the loading dock. A truck pulled in. I was drinking coffee. Hey! A guy needs to relax. Anyway, a truck pulled in when I wasn't looking. The truck bumped a stack of boxes on the dock. One box fell on my foot. My co-worker, Jack Smith, called for help right away. Jack is a great guy. I was taken to Mount Eden Hospital and treated for a broken foot. What bad luck!

### When You Are Treated Unfairly

You may think you are being treated unfairly, or discriminated against, on your job. You cannot seem to solve the problem. Write a letter to the Equal Employment Opportunity Commission, 1801 L Street, N.W., Washington, DC 20507. If you wish to call, dial 1-800-669-4000.

## SKILL 12.4 Communicate with Customers

Marcia is a salesperson in a music store. A customer comes in. He slams a compact disc down on the counter. "You people are crooks," he screams at Marcia. "This stupid CD skips. I ought to turn you in to the Better Business Bureau."

Marcia should probably take a deep breath and say, "Let's see if we can solve this problem."

If this is what you would do, you already understand the first step in working with customers. Most of the time, it is easy to communicate with customers. You find out what they want. You try to be helpful. You smile and do your job well.

With an angry customer, you must use all your skills as a good communicator. Do not take the customer's anger personally. The customer is not really angry with you. He or she is angry about something that happened.

If you start shouting back, the problem will only get worse. If you get very upset and refuse to talk to the customer, you will not be doing your job. Stay calm. Nod your head to show that you are listening to the customer. Talk in a clear, strong voice. Always stay focused on solving the problem. If the situation gets out of hand, get your boss or another co-worker to help you.

**English and Careers**

When you decide to leave a job, write a letter of resignation. State that you are leaving, and tell what your final day will be. It is fine to include the reasons you are moving on. But try to not leave any hard feelings behind.

## Practice

Use a separate sheet of paper to answer these questions.

1. What are three jobs that include dealing with customers?
2. What kind of body language should you use with customers?
3. What is the best way to handle an angry customer?

Chapter

# 12 Review

## Summary


Communicating takes place all the time on the job. Being a good communicator can help solve problems and make your job easier.

Outlines help you prepare for written or spoken communication. An outline has a topic sentence, supporting sentences, and a closing.

Most business writing should be short and to the point. Use complete sentences, easy words, and check your spelling on final drafts. Talk about facts, not feelings.

Communicating with customers is a skill. Always stay calm, listen, and be friendly—even with angry customers.


| |
|---|
| communication |
| presentation |
| memo |
| topic sentence |

## Vocabulary Review

**Match each term in the box with its meaning. Write the term and its matching number on a separate sheet of paper.**

1. a sentence that introduces the subject or states the purpose
2. the giving and receiving of information
3. the act of showing or explaining ideas to another person or group
4. a short note

## Chapter Quiz

**Answer the following questions in one or two sentences. Use a separate sheet of paper.**

1. What is communication?
2. What is an example of a topic sentence?
3. What are two supporting sentences that tell about the topic sentence in Question 2?
4. What is an example of a closing sentence that could complete your outline?
5. Why is it a good idea to write an outline before you give a presentation in person?
6. What is a memo?
7. Which is better business writing: being short and to the point, or using long words and sentences? Explain.
8. What are three things you should do when communicating with an angry customer?

## Critical Thinking

Many times, companies have policies about how you should communicate with customers. How could you find out about this policy?

### Group Activity

Work with a group to perform a skit between a desk clerk at a hotel and someone who is on vacation at the hotel. The desk clerk is rude to the guest. The guest demands to see the manager. What does the manager do?

# Unit 3 Review

**Read each sentence below. Then choose the letter that best completes each one.**

**1.** A good place to look for a new job is in

A. a phone book.
B. the "Want Ads" in a newspaper.
C. neighborhood bulletin boards.
D. all of the above

**2.** It is important to edit your résumé because

A. a résumé takes the place of a cover letter.
B. employers expect to receive several different drafts of your résumé.
C. it gives you a chance to add details that show your skills in a better way.
D. a résumé is always the only way of applying for a job.

**3.** All of the following are ways to use body language in an interview, except

A. make eye contact.
B. smile occasionally.
C. point and cross your arms.
D. keep your feet on the floor and your legs together.

**4.** An employee handbook often gives you information about all of the following, except

A. company policies.
B. rates of pay for everyone in the company.
C. worker benefits.
D. company departments and what they do.

**5.** All of the following are job aids, except a

A. "How-To" list.
B. work schedule.
C. telephone message form.
D. flyer about an after-hours barbecue.

**6.** An outline should always include

A. a photograph.
B. a topic sentence.
C. color-coded tabs.
D. none of the above

**Critical Thinking**

Why is it important to make a good impression when you apply for and begin a new job?

**WRITING** Write a short essay explaining how three of the job skills you learned about in this unit can help you find and keep a good job. Use examples from your own life. Your essay should be at least three paragraphs long.

Unit 4

# English for Independent Living

## Chapter 13
## Finding a Place to Live

## Chapter 14
## Getting Around

## Chapter 15
## Managing Money

*Moving is the last step when getting an apartment. English skills help you find an apartment, fill out an application, and sign a lease.*

# Chapter 13 Finding a Place to Live

## Words to Know

| | |
|---|---|
| **landlord** | a person who owns rental property |
| **credit reference** | a person or business that can vouch that you pay your bills |
| **personal reference** | a person who can speak in favor of another person's good character |
| **vouch** | to speak in favor of; to say that something is true |
| **tenant** | a renter |
| **not applicable** | does not apply |
| **lease** | a written contract between a landlord and a tenant |
| **obligated** | having responsibility for something |
| **utilities** | services, such as gas, electricity, and water |
| **refundable deposit** | money that can be returned if certain conditions are met |

## Interview Project

What would your ideal apartment be? Use the *Who, What, Why, Where, When,* and *How* questions to write an interview guide to help you look for an apartment. Then work with a partner to role-play a scene between a landlord and someone looking for an apartment. Use your interview guide during your role-play. Switch roles.

## Learning Objectives

- Use a list of pros and cons to compare different living situations.
- Find key information in rental ads.
- Write an interview guide for landlords.
- Fill out a rental application.
- Find key words and phrases in a lease.

## SKILL 13.1 List Pros and Cons of Living Situations

At one time, most American adults expected to finish school, get a job, and buy a house. In today's housing market, fewer people can afford to buy a house. More people are finding they must choose to

- rent an apartment on their own.
- rent an apartment and share it with roommates.
- rent a room in a house and share the kitchen.

There are pros and cons to each of these situations. Use your English skills to outline them. Here is a list of one person's pros and cons for renting an apartment without roommates.

**Everyday English**

How could you use lists of pros and cons to decide which neighborhood is best for you?

*Pros*

1. *Privacy*
2. *Don't have to clean up other people's messes*
3. *Don't have to worry about roommates not paying bills*

*Cons*

1. *Can get lonely*
2. *Have to pay all the bills myself*
3. *No one to feed my cat when I'm out of town*

Listing the pros and cons helps you make a comparison. You can then make a decision based on your values. You might decide that roommates are too much trouble. You might decide that you will work things out with a roommate to have company and save money.

## Practice

On a separate sheet of paper, list at least three pros and cons for each of the three living situations listed on page 152. Then decide which arrangement best suits your needs.

## SKILL 13.2 Read Rental Ads

A good way to find a place is to look in the "For Rent" ads of the newspaper. Like "Want Ads" for employment, "For Rent" ads are found in the Classifieds section of the newspaper. Rental ads are organized in different ways. Usually, you will find the following groupings.

- Apartments for Rent
- Roommates Wanted
- Houses to Share

Newspapers often list rental apartments by neighborhood as well. Suppose you need an apartment close to your job. First see if there are separate rental listings for that part of town.

### Abbreviations in Rental Ads

In Chapter 7, you learned some abbreviations to help you understand "Want Ads." On the next page are some special abbreviations to learn for rental ads.

**English and Technology**

The Internet is a helpful tool in the search for an apartment. You can find local and national rental ads. These are usually links from your local newspaper's Web site.

| | |
|---|---|
| apt. | apartment |
| ba. | bath |
| br. | bedroom |
| frn. | furnished |
| incl. | included |
| lg. | large |
| lndry. | laundry |
| kit. | kitchen |
| nr. trans. | near transportation |
| prkng. | parking |
| rm. | room |
| sec. dep. | security deposit |
| unfrn. | unfurnished |
| util. | utilities |
| w/w cpt. | wall-to-wall carpeting |
| yd. | yard |

## Practice

Complete the following activities on a separate sheet of paper.

**1.** Write this rental ad without abbreviations.

> 2 br. apt., unfrn., lndry, lg. yd., $650 plus util.
> 555-0003

**2.** You want to rent out a room in your two-bedroom apartment. Write a rental ad asking for a roommate. Use abbreviations to keep the ad under 15 words. Remember that each abbreviation stands for one word.

## SKILL 13.3 Interview Your Landlord

Once you find an interesting place in the rental ads, you can call the listed phone number. To save time and energy, prepare an interview guide to use over the phone. Think about a living situation that would be ideal for you. Talk to the **landlord,** or the person who owns the property. Then ask key questions. To write an interview guide, follow these steps.

1. Think about your needs.
2. Use the words *who, what, why, where, when,* and *how* to form questions. Write them down.
3. Make several copies of the guide. Each time you call about an apartment, take notes about it.
4. Write a list of pros and cons to help you decide which apartments you really want to look at.

Here is an example of one person's interview guide.

Address: ____________________

Apartment Number: __________

Phone Number: ____________

Person Called: _____________

Date: ______________________

1. How big is the apartment? __________
2. How many bedrooms does it have? ________
3. How many bathrooms does it have? ________
4. What kind of neighborhood is it in? ________
5. What is the building like? __________
6. How close is it to the 51 bus line? ________
7. Where is the nearest grocery store? ______
8. Where is the closest park? __________

## Practice

Write your own interview guide. Include key things you want to know about an apartment before you take the time to look at it. Do you have a dog? Then you will have to ask if pets are allowed. Do you need a garage? Will an open parking space do? Write at least five questions on a separate sheet of paper.

## SKILL 13.4 Apply for an Apartment

You go to look at an apartment. It seems right for you, but there are three other people there who want it, too. The landlord asks each person to fill out a rental application.

**Brush Up on the Basics**

When filling out a rental application, remember to capitalize proper nouns and adjectives. (See Capitalization 15–16 in the Reference Guide.)

Just as job applications should be filled out neatly, rental applications should also be neat. Most of the time, you will need to fill out an application while you are there. Here is how you can be prepared.

- Bring a sharp pencil and an eraser.
- Bring a list of **credit references** and a list of **personal references.** These people should be able to **vouch** for, or speak in favor of, you or say that you pay your bills and will make a good **tenant,** or renter.
- If you have a driver's license, bring it with you. You may need to write down the license number on the rental application.
- Read the form carefully. Fill in all the blanks. If something does not apply to you, write *N/A*. It stands for **not applicable**, or does not apply.

## Practice

On this page is a sample rental application. Make a copy of it and fill it out.

Charles Lever Properties
P.O. Box 16622
Derry, LA 71421
(318) 555-3002

Charles Lever PROPERTIES

### Rental Application Form

Name: ____________________________________________
(last) (first) (middle initial)

Address: ____________________________________________

____________________________________________

Phone: ____________________________________________

How long at present address? ______________________

Employer: ____________________________________________

Employer Address: ______________________________

____________________________________________

How long at present job? ____________ Income: ____________

Credit Reference: ____________ Phone: ____________

Personal Reference: ____________ Phone: ____________

Do you plan to share this apartment with anyone? Yes___ No___

If yes, give the person's name. ______________________

Do you have any pets? Yes___ No___ If yes, what kind? ____________

I authorize owner/agent to verify the above information, including but not limited to obtaining a credit report.

Signature ______________________ Date: ______________

## SKILL 13.5 Sign a Lease

Often, after being approved for an apartment, you will have to sign a **lease.** A lease is a legal contract. It outlines the agreement between you and your landlord.

**English Tip**
When you move into an apartment, take notes on anything that is already damaged. Keep one copy and give one copy to your landlord.

Leases may be very simple and easy to understand. Sometimes they may be long, written in small print, and full of difficult legal terms. Before you sign a lease, you should read it carefully. You should make notes about anything you do not understand. Then you should get those questions answered. Here are some key pieces of information that should be included in the lease.

- The time period the lease covers. Some leases are month-to-month. Other leases last for six months to a year. While the lease is in effect, the landlord cannot raise the rent. You are **obligated,** or required, to stay for that whole period. When the lease is up, the landlord can legally ask you to leave. The landlord can also increase your rent or make other changes in any terms of the lease.
- Who pays for **utilities,** such as gas, electricity, and water? Sometimes the landlord pays for gas and electricity. Sometimes landlords just pay for garbage collection and water. Make sure you know exactly what you are paying for.
- First and last months' rents. Some landlords want you to pay two months' rent in advance. They do this in case you leave without notice or do not pay your rent.

- The security deposit. You may have to pay a security deposit. This is an amount of money the landlord keeps if you damage the apartment. If you leave the apartment in good condition, this money is returned to you. This is called a **refundable deposit.**
- The cleaning deposit. This fee is usually not refundable. It is used to clean and paint the apartment after you are gone. Make sure you ask your landlord how this deposit is different from a security deposit.

**Everyday English**

What do you think people mean when they say, "Read the fine print"?

## Practice

Write one or two sentences explaining the following words or phrases. They might be found on a lease. Write your answers on a separate sheet of paper.

**1.** month-to-month

**2.** $75 cleaning fee

**3.** first and last months' rents

**4.** security deposit due upon moving in

**5.** landlord pays for all utilities

Chapter

# 13 Review

## Summary

A list of pros and cons can help you compare living situations.

The newspaper rental ads section is a good place to find rentals. Rental ads can be organized by type of living situation and neighborhood. Rental ads usually use abbreviations to describe apartments.

Writing an interview guide can help you learn more about apartments over the phone. You can then decide if the apartments are worth looking at.

Rental applications often need to be filled out when you look at an apartment. Neatness counts.

Leases should be read carefully. Look for key words and phrases. Know what you are signing.

| |
|---|
| obligated |
| vouch |
| lease |
| landlord |
| personal references |
| credit reference |

## Vocabulary Review

**Complete each sentence with a term from the box. Use a separate sheet of paper.**

1. A ____ is a person who owns rental property.
2. When looking for an apartment, you should always bring a list of credit references and ____ with you.
3. To ____ for someone is to speak in favor of them.
4. A legal contract that outlines an agreement between a landlord and tenant is called a ____.
5. A person or business that can vouch that you pay your bills is called a ____.
6. When you have responsibility for something, you are ____.

## Chapter Quiz

**Answer the following questions in one or two sentences. Use a separate sheet of paper.**

1. How can lists of pros and cons help you find a place to live?
2. What does each of the following abbreviations mean: *ba., nr. trans., util., lndry.*?
3. How can rental ads grouped by neighborhood help you find a place suited for you?
4. What are three questions you might include on a landlord interview guide?
5. How can using an interview guide save you time?
6. What are two things you should bring with you to fill out a rental application?
7. Why is it important to be prepared to fill out a rental application on the spot?
8. What is a lease?
9. How are a security deposit and a cleaning fee different?
10. Suppose a lease is long and hard to read. Should you sign it without doing anything else? Explain.

## Critical Thinking

How could a library help you learn more about leases?

### Group Activity

Work with your group to write a list of five things a person should consider before renting an apartment. Then share your list with another group. Edit your list to include items from the other group's.

*People use English skills to find and use public transportation. Reading a bus or train schedule is like reading a chart.*

# Chapter 14 Getting Around

## Words to Know

| | |
|---|---|
| **public transportation** | vehicles like buses and subways that are available for anyone to use |
| **car pool** | a group of people who share car rides |
| **route** | a certain path or direction |
| **points of interest** | interesting things to do and see |
| **intersection** | the place where two streets cross each other |

## Mapping Project

Draw a map of your school. Label the important places, such as the principal's office, the gym, and the cafeteria. Then make a grid. On the left-hand side of your map, write the letters *A, B, C, D,* and *E* one inch apart. Across the top of your map, write the numbers *1, 2, 3, 4,* and *5* one inch apart. Draw lines down and across the map. Then write an index that explains what your map shows.

## Learning Objectives

- Use a telephone book to learn about public transportation.
- Read a bus schedule.
- Use a street index and map.
- Interpret road signs.
- Describe three steps in studying for a driver's test.

## SKILL 14.1 Find Public Transportation

Your city probably has some type of **public transportation** that anyone can use. Most kinds of public transportation are paid for with the help of tax dollars. This helps keep the cost of using them low. The most common type of public transportation is the bus. Some large cities also have underground trains or subways. In San Francisco, ferries carry workers across the bay.

> **English and Technology**
>
> Many public transportation companies have Web sites with information about schedules, stops, and fares.

How do you find public transportation? Use a telephone book. Begin by looking in the front of the white pages. Under government listings, find a general information number for your city or county. If you know the name of the transportation system, look in the white pages under that name.

In addition, many cities and counties are starting **car pool** agencies. These agencies try to match cars and riders. People sharing rides saves money and makes highways less crowded.

## Practice

Complete the following activities on a separate sheet of paper.

1. You need to know about buses that run through the north side of your city. Make a list of at least three questions you could ask when you call the bus company.
2. Write a list of pros and cons about using public transportation.
3. If the bus system in your city was called Tran-Sit, how would you find it in a phone book?

## SKILL 14.2 Read a Bus Schedule

Phil picked up a bus schedule from a counter at a library, but he was not sure how to read it.

Reading a bus schedule is like reading any table or chart. Look at the bus schedule on page 166. It shows the different stops on the bus **route**, or path. The bus stops are in order. For example, the first stop is Westlake Drive. The second stop is Oakwood Avenue, and so on.

**English Tip**
If you have trouble understanding a bus or train schedule, ask a public transportation worker for help.

Each row of times next to the bus stops tells you what time you can catch the bus there. The bus stops at Westlake Drive at 5:51 A.M., 6:08 A.M., 6:42 A.M., and 7:02 A.M.

You need to know the street the bus is traveling on, too. A map of the route is often included on a bus schedule so you will know right where the bus stops on Westlake Drive, Oakwood Avenue, and so on.

Now, suppose you are getting on the bus at Westlake Drive. Your job interview is near the Elm Street stop. You can find out how long it will take you to get to Elm Street by studying the columns. Follow these steps using the bus schedule on the next page.

**Step 1:**
Suppose you are getting on the Westlake Drive stop at 7:02 A.M. Put your finger on the column where 7:02 A.M. begins.

**Step 2:**
Run your finger down that column until you are pointing to the Elm Street stop.

**Step 3:**
Your finger should be on 7:38 A.M. Subtract 7:02 from 7:38. You can see that it will take you 36 minutes to get to Elm Street.

| Bus Stop: | Time: | | | |
|---|---|---|---|---|
| Westlake Dr. | 5:51 A.M. | 6:08 A.M. | 6:42 A.M. | 7:02 A.M. |
| Oakwood Ave. | 5:58 A.M. | 6:16 A.M. | 6:50 A.M. | 7:10 A.M. |
| Fruitvale St. | 6:04 A.M. | 6:25 A.M. | 6:58 A.M. | 7:18 A.M. |
| Sunset Blvd. | 6:12 A.M. | 6:37 A.M. | 7:08 A.M. | 7:26 A.M. |
| Elm St. | 6:20 A.M. | 6:48 A.M. | 7:19 A.M. | 7:38 A.M. |

*Sample bus schedule*

## Practice

Use a separate sheet of paper to answer the following questions. Use the bus schedule above.

1. You need to be on Elm Street by 7:30 A.M. What is the latest time you can get on the bus at Westlake Drive?

2. What stops are between Westlake Drive and Sunset Boulevard?

3. What is the earliest time you can catch a bus on Fruitvale Street?

## SKILL 14.3 Use a Street Index

Whether you are driving a car or taking the bus, it is good to know how to use a street index. Street indexes are on maps. You can use a street index to find streets. You can also use it to find interesting things to do and see. On a street index, these interesting things are called **points of interest.**

A street index is like the index of a book. It has several headings with alphabetical listings below it. Here are some examples.

*Parks*

Children's Park A-1

Hobie's Park Q-7

*Points of Interest*

City Hall D-3

City Zoo X-7

*Streets*

Baker Street C-2

Bush Street E-2

Heart Street B-3

Henry Street C-2

Jones Street A-2

Martin Luther King, Jr., Way A-4

Parker Street B-2

Penny Street A-1

You can see the letters and numbers after each listing. These tell you how to find what you are looking for on a map. Look at the map on page 168.

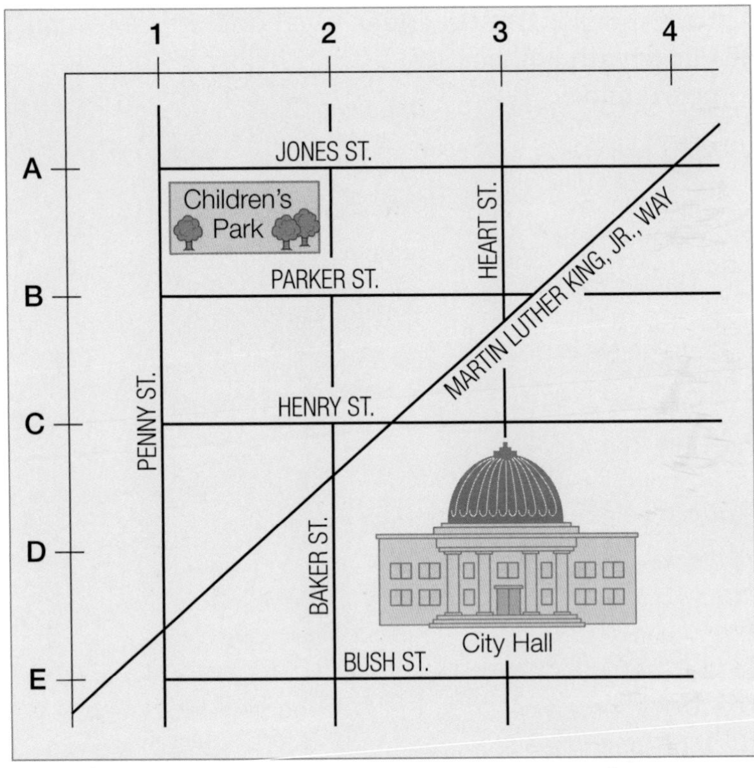


***Downtown map***

On the left side of the map are letters. Along the top of the map are numbers. Suppose you want to find Martin Luther King, Jr., Way. The street index lists it as A-4. To find this street, put one finger on the letter A. Move your finger across the map until it is under the number 4. Your finger is at the **intersection** of Martin Luther King, Jr., Way and Jones Street. That is the place where the two streets cross.

Large city maps index hundreds of streets and points of interest. Knowing how to use the index is a good way to get to know your city.

## Practice

Look at the index on page 167 and the map on page 168. Then use a separate sheet of paper to answer the following questions.

1. What intersection is at point C-2 on the map?
2. What points of interest are on the map?
3. How would you use the index to find Bush Street?

## SKILL 14.4 Interpret Road Signs

Now that Maria is on her own, she has decided to buy a car. She is going to use all the English skills she learned in Units One and Two to get a great deal on a car. Does she have the English skills she needs to get a driver's license?

Most people do not connect English skills and driving. How would you like to be on the road with someone who could not read road signs?

*Black and white road signs tell you what to do. You must read them carefully when you are driving.*

**Everyday English**

Do you know what the word *yield* means on a sign? If you need help, use a dictionary or ask a friend.

Of course, some signs do not have any words. It is the driver's job to know what those signs stand for. Here are some examples.

*This sign tells you there is a traffic light ahead.*

*This sign tells you that an intersection is coming up.*

## Practice

On a separate sheet of paper, write what you think each of these signs means.

**1.** **2.**

## SKILL 14.5 Study for Your Driver's Test

To get a driver's license, you usually have to take two tests. One is a test of your driving ability. You will have to drive a car with an examiner riding with you, watching what you do. The other is a written, multiple-choice test. This test focuses on laws and driving procedures. Most state motor vehicle departments have a book you can use to study for the written test.

**Brush Up on the Basics**

Pay special attention to prepositions as you study your driver's test. Prepositions such as *on, in, over,* and *under* often show distance and direction. (See Grammar 48 in the Reference Guide.)

Once you get your driving book, here is what you should do.

1. Read it in small sections. You will remember more if you study a little each day.
2. Take notes on what you read. Look for key words.
3. Before you take the test, look back over the suggestions for taking objective tests. You will find them in Chapter 4, on page 49.
4. If you fail the test, ask if you can keep it. Take the test home and study the answers you got wrong. Then take the test again when you are ready.

To apply for a driver's license, you will need to have some identification with you. This will usually be your birth certificate and social security card. How do you find the state Department of Motor Vehicles office nearest you? Look in the state government section of your phone book.

Many states require you to get a learner's permit before you apply for a driver's license. A learner's permit allows you to drive a car only when a licensed driver is seated beside you. You must always carry this permit with you when you are learning to drive.

Once you pass all the tests, you will have to pay a fee to get your driver's license. Remember that a driver's license is a legal document. If you misplace your license, you can get a copy at the Department of Motor Vehicles. Your license may also be suspended or taken away for a number of reasons. Reckless driving, speeding, and driving under the influence of alcohol or drugs are common reasons for losing a driver's license.

## Practice

Answer the following questions on a separate sheet of paper.

1. How are English skills and driving connected?
2. What are two common road signs, and what do they mean?
3. If you did not know the driving laws in your state, how could you find out about them?
4. How would you go about studying for a driver's license test?
5. How could you find the Department of Motor Vehicles office nearest you?
6. What can you do if you misplace your driver's license?

## Chapter 14 Review

### Summary

| |
|---|
| Information about public transportation can be found in a telephone book. Try city and county governments first for information. |
| Bus schedules tell you the times when buses leave and arrive at certain stops. Reading a schedule is like reading a chart. |
| Most maps have a street index. This index lists streets, points of interest, and more. Numbers and letters on the map help you find indexed streets. |
| Road signs give drivers important information. Make sure you know how to interpret road signs. |
| Driving and English skills go together. Drivers must read written signs and understand the meanings of picture signs. They must also study for a written driver's test. |

| |
|---|
| public transportation |
| route |
| car pool |
| points of interest |
| intersection |

### Vocabulary Review

**Match each term in the box with its meaning. Write the term and its matching number on a separate sheet of paper.**

1. interesting things to do and see
2. people who share car rides
3. place where two roads cross
4. transportation anyone can use
5. a certain path or direction

## Chapter Quiz

**Answer the following questions in one or two sentences. Use a separate sheet of paper.**

1. What are two pros and two cons for using public transportation?
2. You are new in a city. How would you go about finding public transportation?
3. What information is on a bus schedule?
4. Jessica is on vacation. How can a map help her find interesting things to see in the city she is visiting?
5. How do the numbers and letters on a street index help a person find streets?
6. What two kinds of tests must a person take to get a driver's license?
7. What are three steps in studying for a written driver's license test?

## Critical Thinking

**On a separate sheet of paper, take notes on this paragraph. Then answer the question that follows.**

> State law says you must never drive faster than is safe for the present conditions. Do not go by the speed limit sign. Weather conditions, the amount of traffic, and other things can make driving at the speed limit dangerous.

Can you always drive the speed limit safely? Explain.

### Group Activity

Work with your group to design a poster about driver safety. Include illustrations of road signs. List ways that drivers can be safer. Then share your poster with the class.

*It is a good idea to shop around before you open a checking account. Knowing key words for banking will help you find the best deal and manage your money.*

# Chapter 15 Managing Money

## Words to Know

| | |
|---|---|
| **deposit** | money that is put in an account; to put money in an account |
| **minimum** | the least amount |
| **balance** | an amount |
| **interest** | the percentage earned or charged on money |
| **check register** | a record book for checks |
| **transaction** | an exchange, usually involving money |
| **annual fee** | a yearly charge |

### Writing Project

Why is it important to have good English skills to manage money? Use an outline to help you answer this question as you read the chapter. Then review your outline and write three paragraphs about how good English skills can help you manage your money better.

### Learning Objectives

- Write an interview guide for banking.
- Write a check.
- Fill in a check register.
- Describe how to get a credit card.
- Identify key items on bills.

## SKILL 15.1 Write an Interview Guide

**English and Technology**

Some computer software programs let you balance your checkbook electronically. Some banks let you pay bills online.

An important part of living on your own is having a checking account. Checking accounts can make your life easier. You do not have to carry large amounts of cash around. You can mail in checks to pay your bills. You can **deposit** your paycheck in the account and know that the money is safe.

You can open a checking account at a bank, a savings and loan association, or a credit union. Some people think that these organizations are run by the government. They are not. They are businesses just like the corner store. They stay in business because you pay them to take care of your money.

For this reason, it is a good idea to shop around for a checking account. You can begin by writing an interview guide with the *who, what, why, where, when,* and *how* questions. Here are some key words to help you write the guide.

### Minimum deposit

Most banks want you to start the account with a certain amount of money. This is called the **minimum** deposit. Find out what this minimum deposit amount is for each bank you interview.

### Check printing fee

Some banks charge you for printing checks. Other banks give you free checks.

### Monthly service charges

Banks often charge a monthly fee just to keep your account open. They take this amount out of your account as a service charge. Sometimes they also charge you for each check you write.

### Minimum balance

Sometimes banks want you to keep a certain amount of money in your account. This is called a minimum **balance.** If you go below that amount, the bank might charge you extra fees. Sometimes, the bank may close your account.

### Interest

Some banks pay you **interest** on your checking account. This means that you earn a certain amount of money based on the amount in your account. Here is an example. You have $100 in your checking account. The bank says it will pay you 2% annual interest on it. This comes to .17% interest each month. At the end of the month, the bank adds 17 cents to your account. You have earned 17 cents in interest in one month.

Use your interview guide with several banks. Take notes, and compare what you find out. Then choose the bank that gives you a good deal, has convenient hours, and offers many services.

## Practice

Use a separate sheet of paper to answer these questions.

1. What are three questions to ask a bank representative when shopping around for a checking account?

2. Keyshawn interviewed two banks. The first bank offered a checking account with no minimum balance required. There was a monthly fee of $5.50, and a 20-cent charge for each check he writes. The second bank offered an account with no monthly fee and no per-check charge. Keyshawn must keep a minimum balance of $500. If he goes below that amount, the bank will charge him $20 a month. Keyshawn has $500. What should he do?

## SKILL 15.2 Fill Out a Check

Once you get your checking account, you will receive your own set of checks. Each check will have your name, address, and account number already printed on it. To write a check, just fill in the blanks. Study the filled-out check below.

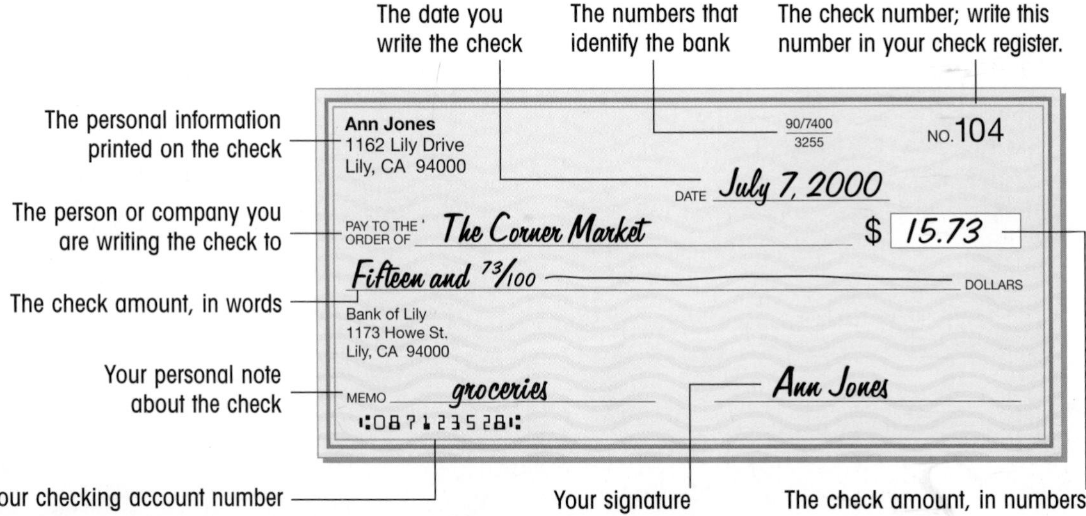

## Practice

Use a separate sheet of paper to answer the following questions, based on the check on page 180.

1. Where is the checking account number of Ann Jones's check?
2. What personal information is printed on the check?
3. Where can you find the check number?
4. How should you write a check? On a separate sheet of paper, draw a blank check. Fill it in. Pay $20.00 (twenty dollars) to a friend. Make a personal note that you are paying back a loan.

### Everyday English

Once your check is signed, it can be cashed. Sign it only after all the other information is filled in.

## SKILL 15.3 Use a Check Register

Once you write a check, you should record the information in your **check register.** This is a record that comes with your checkbook. The check register is like a chart or table. You simply look at the heading of each column. Then you fill in the information. The check register entry below is for the check shown on page 180.

| NUMBER | DATE | DESCRIPTION OF TRANSACTION | (-) PAYMENT | FEE (IF ANY) | (+) DEPOSIT | BALANCE $ 161.03 |
|---|---|---|---|---|---|---|
| 104 | 7/7/00 | The Corner Market | 15.73 | – | – | 145.30 |
| | | | | | | |
| | | | | | | |

**Brush Up on the Basics**

When you write a check, use a hyphen (-) in compound numbers from twenty-one to ninety-nine. (See Punctuation 23 in the Reference Guide.)

You can learn a few things from Ann Jones's check register. The word **transaction** refers to what took place. Notice that Ann Jones did not write in a fee. This is because she is not charged by her bank for writing checks. If Ann deposits money, she will record the amount in the register as well.

## Practice

Ann deposits $90.00 into her account on May 15, 2000. On a separate sheet of paper, show what her check register would look like.

## SKILL 15.4 Know Key Words for Credit Cards

The time will come when you get an offer in the mail. It will read something like this:

> We are saving a credit card with your name on it. Just fill in the application and send it back to us. Charge up to $1,500 on your new Best Credit Card.

It sounds great. Buy now, pay later. However, before you sign up for a credit card, put some of your English skills to work. Here are some key words to look for when you are considering using a credit card.

### Annual fee

Credit card companies, like banks, make money when you use their services. Most credit cards charge you an **annual fee.** This is a yearly charge that you must pay the company. It is often between $10 and $30 per year.

### Interest

Credit card companies make most of their money by charging you interest. Here is how credit card interest works.

You buy a suit for $200 using your credit card. When the bill comes, you do not have the money to pay it. "I'll wait until next month," you might say to yourself.

The next month, your bill is $203.00. The credit card company charged you 18% annual interest on the $200.00. This comes to $1\frac{1}{2}$% interest per month. Now you owe even more. If you did not make any payment the month before, you will probably have to pay an extra $25.00 as a late fee.

Credit cards can be good to have. They come in handy during emergencies. When you apply for one, you should know exactly what you are signing up for. Read the small print on letters that invite you to get credit cards. Read applications carefully. Find out what the annual fee and annual interest are. Each time you use the card, remember that a bill is coming later in the month!

**English Tip**

You have to read letters from credit card companies carefully to find information on fees and interest. Often, this information is in very small print. Why do you think credit card companies do this?

## Practice

Use a separate sheet of paper to answer the following questions.

1. What is a credit card?
2. Mariah gets a letter inviting her to apply for a credit card. What two key pieces of information should she look for in the letter?
3. What are two pros and two cons of using credit cards?

## SKILL 15.5 Read Bills

When you are living on your own, that credit card bill is not the only bill you may receive. Most likely, you will get phone bills, electricity bills, and gas bills. If you own a home, you will get tax bills.

When you get a bill, use your English skills to read it carefully. Sometimes companies make mistakes when they prepare your bill. It is up to you to make sure the bills are correct. If they are not, it is up to you to get them corrected.

Here are some key phrases to look for when you read a bill.

### Total amount due or balance

This is the amount of money you owe the company.

### Explanation of charges

Companies break down the amount on a bill to show exactly what you have been charged for. The telephone company, for example, will list each of your long distance calls. The gas company will show you how much energy you used. A credit card company will list each item you charged. Read these items carefully. It is the only way to know whether you are being charged the right amount.

### Previous balance

This shows the amount you owed before this new bill. If it has not been paid, it will be added to your current charges.

### Payments made

Here the business shows how much you have paid on your account since you were last billed. Look to see that your last payment has been deducted from your previous balance.

### Taxes, interest, service fees

These are extra charges added to your bill.

### Due date

Somewhere on the bill is a due date. If you do not pay the bill by that date, you may be charged extra.

### Account number

This is the number a business uses to keep track of each customer. If you have a question about your bill, this is the number you use to identify yourself.

Bills will often list a phone number you can call if you have questions about charges. Don't hesitate to use it! Have your account number, questions, and note pad ready when you call.

No two bills are alike. You must study each bill carefully to find the information you are looking for. It is well worth the trouble.

## Practice

Study this phone bill. Then answer the questions below.

| | **Jayson Elliot**<br>**123 Samson Court**<br>**Oakland, CA 94605** | | | | **Account Number: 000-000-1111**<br>**Statement Date: Oct. 5, 2000** | | | Page 1 |
|---|---|---|---|---|---|---|---|---|
| Account Summary | Previous bill | | | | | | 18.34 | |
| | Payments applied through Sept. 7, 2000 | | | | | | 18.34CR | |
| | Balance ***Thank You for Your Payment*** | | | | | | | .00 |
| | Current charges: | | | | | | | |
| | Pacific Bell (Page 2) | | | | | | | |
| | CURRENT CHARGES DUE BY Nov. 5, 2000 | | | | | | | 20.16 |
| **Total Due** | | | | | | | | **$20.16** |
| | Item | Date | Time | Min* | Place and Number Called | | | Charge |
| Calls | 1 | Sep 8 | 957A | 4 DD | BERKELEY | CA | 415 555 6903 | .97 |
| | 2 | Sep 21 | 932A | 4 DD | BERKELEY | CA | 415 555 6903 | .97 |
| | 3 | Sep 23 | 918A | 1 DD | BERKELEY | CA | 415 555 6902 | .31 |
| | 4 | Sep 23 | 438P | 5 DD | BERKELEY | CA | 415 555 6902 | 1.19 |
| | 5 | Sep 29 | 1137A | 1 DD | SAN FRAN | CA | 415 555 9476 | .34 |
| | * See Rate Key on Reverse | | | | | | | |
| | | | | | Subtotal | | | $3.78 |
| | Item | | | | | | | Charge |
| Monthly Charges | 12 | Basic Monthly Service Charge | | | | | | 15.83 |
| | 13 | Tax: | Fed: .47 | | 911: .08 | | | .55 |
| | Monthly Charges | | | | Subtotal | | | $16.38 |
| **Total Due** | **Current Charges** | | | | | | | **$20.16** |

1. How much money does Jayson owe?
2. How much of the total bill is for phone calls?
3. How much of the total bill is for monthly charges?
4. How much does Jayson pay in federal taxes?
5. How much does Jayson pay for the 911 service tax?
6. How much was Jayson's bill the previous month?
7. When is this phone bill due?

Telephone costs can add up quickly. Calls from a cell phone or a pay phone usually cost more than calls from a home or business phone. For example, compare these weekday rates for a 3-minute call from San Francisco, California, to some other cities.

| Unassisted 3-Minute Call | | | | |
|---|---|---|---|---|
| From San Francisco to: | Distance | Home Phone Rate | Pay Phone Rate | Cell Phone Rate |
| Hayward | 30 miles | $.30 | $1.20 | $1.35 |
| Santa Rosa | 60 miles | .45 | 1.50 | 2.25 |
| New York City | 3,000 miles | .45 | 1.50 | 3.50 |

## Practice

Use the table above to answer these questions. Write your answers on a separate sheet of paper.

1. How much more would it cost to call Hayward on a pay phone than on a home phone?

2. How much more would it cost to call Santa Rosa on a cell phone than on a home phone?

3. How much more would it cost to call New York City on a cell phone than on a home phone?

4. What is the distance from San Francisco to New York City?

5. What is the pay phone rate from San Francisco to Santa Rosa?

Chapter

# 15 Review

## Summary

| |
|---|
| English skills can help you keep track of your money. |
| Use an interview guide to shop for the best checking account. |
| Fill out checks completely and carefully. Sign your name to the check only after it is filled out. |
| Fill out the check register as you would any chart. It will help you keep track of the amount of money in your account. |
| Look for the annual fee and interest when applying for a credit card. |
| Read bills carefully to make sure you are being charged the right amount. |

| |
|---|
| deposit |
| minimum |
| transaction |
| balance |
| annual fee |

## Vocabulary Review

**Match each term in the box with its meaning. Write the term and its matching number on a separate sheet of paper.**

1. a yearly charge
2. an exchange, usually involving money
3. an amount
4. the least amount
5. money that is put in an account; to put money in an account

## Chapter Quiz

**Answer the following questions in one or two sentences. Use a separate sheet of paper.**

1. What are two reasons to have a checking account?
2. What are three questions you might put on your interview guide for checking accounts?
3. What are two fees a bank might charge?
4. What does *minimum balance* mean?
5. What are the seven column headings on a check register?
6. What is an *annual service fee* for a credit card?
7. Why should you read the small print on a credit card application?
8. Why should you read your bills carefully?
9. Suppose you have a question about your bill. How do you know where to call?
10. How do you know when to pay your bill?

## Critical Thinking

Your friend needs to start a checking account. She visits one bank and tells you she does not want to visit another bank.

Write a short paragraph in which you explain why your friend should compare at least two banks.

### Group Activity

Work with your group to discuss the pros and cons of having credit cards. Use your ideas to create a list of pros and cons with at least three entries.

# Unit 4 Review

**Read each sentence below. Then choose the letter that best completes each one.**

1. While a lease is in effect,
   A. your rent cannot be raised.
   B. you can stop paying rent if you find a better apartment.
   C. a landlord can raise your rent.
   D. none of the above

2. A bus schedule tells you all of the following, except
   A. the route the bus takes.
   B. the average number of passengers at each stop.
   C. the times when the bus stops.
   D. the places where the bus stops.

3. A street index tells you
   A. how long a street is.
   B. where police cars go during an emergency.
   C. where on a map you can find a certain street.
   D. price information for buying a home.

4. A learner's permit allows you to drive a car
   A. on your own to practice driving.
   B. as long as a licensed driver is also somewhere in the car.
   C. with the permission of a licensed driver.
   D. only when a licensed driver is seated beside you.

5. A check register is used to do all of the following, except
   A. record information about checks you write.
   B. report information to the bank about checks you plan to write.
   C. keep track of fees which a bank charges.
   D. record the amount of money you deposit.

6. Credit card companies sometimes charge you
   A. an annual fee.
   B. a fee for making late payments.
   C. interest on money you owe.
   D. all of the above

**Critical Thinking**

Why is it important to interview your landlord before choosing a place to live?

**WRITING** A lease and a credit card agreement are each legal documents. Choose one and write an essay describing the benefits it brings to you. Also discuss the responsibility you have when you sign the document. Your essay should be at least three paragraphs long.

# Unit 5 English for Citizens

Chapter 16
## Working with the Government

Chapter 17
## Paying Taxes

*English skills help you work with the government. Whether you are voting in an election or applying for a driver's license, you will need to understand what you read.*

Chapter 16

# Working with the Government

## Words to Know

| | |
|---|---|
| **birth certificate** | an official record that contains a person's family and birth information |
| **election** | the choosing of government leaders or local laws by voting |
| **register** | to sign up |
| **proposition** | a local or state law, or issue, that must be voted on |
| **ballot** | a list of people running for office; also a list of local laws that must be voted on |
| **editorial** | a statement of opinion |
| **bias** | an attitude that is strongly or unfairly on one side of an issue |

## Informed Voter Project

List at least five ways you can become an informed voter before you read the chapter. Then as you read the chapter, compare your ideas with the ones in the book. Edit your ideas by adding new ways to be an informed voter.

## Learning Objectives

- Locate key government agencies in a telephone book.
- Fill out government forms.
- Identify examples of bias in campaign materials.
- Learn about candidates and issues to make informed voting decisions.

## SKILL 16.1 Use a Telephone Book

Brandy is applying for a driver's license. She has waited in a long line at the Department of Motor Vehicles. Finally, the clerk asks, "Did you bring proof of your age?" Brandy has brought her mother, who tells the clerk how old Brandy is. The clerk tells Brandy that she needs more proof.

A driver's license or state identification card can be used as proof of age. To get either one of these, you will need your **birth certificate.** A birth certificate is an official city or county government record of when you were born. It also contains family and health information about you. How do you get one?

**English and Careers**

You may need information from government agencies or businesses when you are at work. Knowing where to find listings in a phone book will speed up your search.

To get information from any government agency, start with a telephone book. Most white pages begin with an *Easy Reference List.* This list contains the most-often-used government telephone numbers. Look up the heading "Birth Certificates" or "Birth Records." You will probably find the number you need.

What if an agency is not in the *Easy Reference List*? Ask yourself if the agency is run by the city, county, state, or federal government. Birth certificates are kept by the city or county in which you were born. You would need to look under the city or county government listings.

What if you were born far away from where you are now living? Then you may want to write for information on how to obtain your birth certificate. Suppose you do not know which government—city, county, state, or federal—runs the agency you are looking for. You do not even know the name of the agency. You can scan the listings under all the government agencies. If there is an information number, call it. If you get the wrong agency, tell the person who answers the phone what you want. That person may be able to tell you the right number to call.

**Brush Up on the Basics**

Remember to use a comma (,) after the closing of a business letter. (See Punctuation 13 in the Reference Guide.)

## Practice

Complete the following activities.

1. You want to find the nearest state Department of Motor Vehicles.
   a. Where is the first place you would look?
   b. Where is the second place you would look?

2. The following list is from the *Easy Reference List* of a telephone book. Scan the list and find the telephone number for each item below.
   a. dog licenses in Richmond
   b. boat permits in Oakville
   c. bicycle licenses in Frankville

**LICENSES-PERMITS-REGISTRATIONS**

Auto and Boat Registrations-Plates-Permits

| | |
|---|---|
| Frankville | 555-0098 |
| Oakville | 555-1123 |
| Richmond | 555-1120 |
| Birth and Death | 555-0066 |

(Practice continues on next page.) ➪

(Practice continued.)

| **Business** | |
|---|---|
| Richmond | 555-1110 |
| Franklin | 555-7777 |
| Oakville | 555-0276 |
| Salem | 555-8898 |
| **Bicycle** | |
| Richmond | 555-3342 |
| Frankville | 555-3456 |
| Oakville | 555-7693 |
| **Dog** | |
| Richmond | 555-8664 |
| Oakville | 555-7694 |
| **Marriage** | 555-9999 |

## SKILL 16.2 Fill Out Forms

**Everyday English**

Are you planning to leave the country? You might need a passport. Contact your local postal service for information on how and where to apply.

To apply for any kind of license, you will need to fill out a form. The government needs forms that are completely filled out. An incomplete form might mean you will have to return again.

Whenever you have to fill out a government form, be sure to follow the steps below.

1. Read over the form carefully. If you do not understand a word or a direction, use a dictionary. If you still do not understand it, ask a government worker what it means.

2. Fill out the form completely. Print neatly.

3. Some forms ask for a signature. Sign your name and write the date.

Filling out forms correctly and completely the first time will save you time and energy.

## Practice

**Part A.** In order to vote in a government **election,** you must first **register,** or sign up. Use the Voter Registration Card below to answer the questions on page 198.

# REGISTER TO VOTE

## VOTER INFORMATION

**1.** You must be a citizen of the United States.

**2.** You must be 18 years of age or older at the time of the next election.

**3.** You must NOT be in prison or on parole for the conviction of a felony.

**4.** In order to vote in any specific election, you must be registered 29 days prior to that election. If your affidavit is complete, your registration is effective upon receipt by the county clerk. However, you should not consider yourself registered until you receive a Voter Notification Card. If you do NOT receive a Voter Notification Card, call the county clerk.

**5.** If you wish to vote by absentee ballot, a written application must be on file with the county clerk's office at least 7 days before the election. Elections officials mail absentee ballots in the period 7 to 29 days prior to an election (Elections Code § 3001).

**6.** For election information call the number listed below:

Telephone: (707) 555-6201

*(Practice continues on next page.)* ➪

*(Practice continued.)*

**1.** How old do you have to be to vote? Explain.

**2.** How many days *before* an election must you register?

**3.** Suppose you need information about the election. What number should you call?

**Part B:** Study the sample Voter Registration Form below. Refer to it to complete the activities on page 199.

## VOTER INFORMATION

Are you a U.S. citizen? ☐ Yes ☐ No **If you answered NO, do not complete this form.**

This is an application for a ☐ New Registration ☐ Address Change ☐ Name Change

| 1. Last Name | First Name | Middle Name or Initial | Jr., II, etc. |
|---|---|---|---|

| 2. House Number and Street (Enter new address if changed) | Apt. or Lot # | 3. City or Post Office | 4. Zip Code |
|---|---|---|---|

| 5. Additional Rural or Mailing Address (if necessary) | 6. County where you live |
|---|---|

| 7. Birthdate (MO-DAY-YR) | 8. Birthplace (City and State) | 9. Social Security No. (voluntary) | 10. Phone No. (voluntary) |
|---|---|---|---|

11. ADDRESS CHANGE ONLY – PREVIOUS ADDRESS
Previous House Number and Street

| Previous City or Post Office | County | State |
|---|---|---|

| 12. CHANGE OF NAME ONLY | Former Legal Name | Former Signature |
|---|---|---|

I declare under penalty of election falsification I am a citizen of the United States, will have lived in this state for 30 days immediately preceding the next election, and I will be at least 18 years of age at the time of the general election.

**13. Signature of Applicant**

Date ____/____/____ →
MO DAY YR

FOR BOARD USE ONLY
- City, Village, Twp.
- Ward
- Precinct
- School Dist.
- Cong. Dist.
- Senate Dist.
- House Dist.

Information that will remain confidential and be used only for voter registration purposes: 1) the office where you submit your voter registration application or 2) the fact that you have declined to register. WHOEVER COMMITS ELECTION FALSIFICATION IS GUILTY OF A FELONY OF THE FIFTH DEGREE.

1. Read the form. Make a list of words or directions you do not understand. Use the dictionary to help you find word meanings.

2. On a separate sheet of paper, write all the information you need to include on the form.

## SKILL 16.3 Decide How to Vote

Voting wisely is an important way of working with government. It is a way of making your voice heard. It is a way of taking control.

In most elections, you will be choosing from among several people who are running for different offices. You may also be choosing to vote for or against new state or local laws and taxes. Sometimes these items are called **propositions**, or issues. All these choices are listed on a **ballot.**

Before you cast your vote, you must become informed about the people and issues you will be voting for. Here are some ways to prepare.

- Read voter pamphlets published by the government. These pamphlets present both sides of issues or laws. They do not tell you how to vote.

**English Tip**
If you are not a citizen, you will have to become one before you can vote. The Immigration and Naturalization Service will tell you the steps you must take in order to become a citizen.

- Listen to **editorials**, or statements of people's opinion, on TV. Or read editorials in the newspaper. Also read campaign material put out by committees and parties. Remember that this kind of material is **biased.** It gives one person's or one group's opinion. It is meant to influence your vote. It hardly ever presents both sides of an issue equally.
- As you read campaign material, take notes. List pros and cons. Then make your decision.

## Practice

Here is a letter to the editor that was printed in a local paper. Read it, and then answer the questions on page 201.

**On Proposition A**

If passed, Proposition A would require all businesses in the city to pay a child-care tax. This tax would help run child-care centers in the area. It sounds like a good idea, but think about it.

How will businesses pay for this tax? They will raise prices. New businesses will be less likely to move to our fair city because of this extra tax. This will cost our citizens jobs.

The tax is unfair. Let parents pay for their own child care, and let businesses do what they were meant to do. I hope other citizens will join me in voting against Proposition A.

*—A Concerned Business Owner*

1. What is Proposition A?

2. Does this letter to the editor present both sides of the issue? Explain.

3. List any pros or cons you pick up about this proposition from the letter.

4. Where could you find more information about Proposition A?

### Changes in Voting Laws

States have the right to set qualifications for voters, but they may not discriminate because of race, sex, or age. When the United States was first formed, only free, white males who owned property were allowed to vote. Now every citizen has that right.

Through the years three amendments were added to the Constitution to guarantee the right to vote. The Fifteenth Amendment was passed in 1870. It outlawed discrimination against voters on the basis of race or color. The Nineteenth Amendment was passed in 1920. It gave women the right to vote in all elections. The Twenty-sixth Amendment was passed in 1971. It gave the right to vote to all persons 18 years of age or older.

# Chapter 16 Review

## Summary

The government is part of your everyday life. English skills can help you work smoothly with the government, vote, and take part in government decision making.

Use a telephone book to find government agencies. First, look in the *Easy Reference List.* Then look under the branch of government that runs the agency. Call the government information number for help. Finally, scan the listings for other agencies that may be able to help you.

Fill out forms neatly and completely to save time. If you do not understand something on a form, ask a government worker what it means.

Read about election issues before you vote. Check to see whether what you are reading or listening to is fair. Take notes, list pros and cons, and then decide on your own position.

| |
|---|
| birth certificate |
| ballot |
| register |
| bias |
| editorial |
| proposition |

## Vocabulary Review

**Match each term in the box with its meaning. Write the term and its matching number on a separate sheet of paper.**

1. a list of people running for office
2. a statement of opinion
3. an attitude that is strongly or unfairly on one side of an issue
4. an official record containing a person's family and birth information
5. a local or state law, or issue, that must be voted on
6. to sign up

## Chapter Quiz

**Answer the following questions in one or two sentences. Use a separate sheet of paper.**

1. What are three times in your life you might need to work with a government agency?
2. What are the four levels of government listed in a phone book?
3. You want to complain about the garbage pickup service in your city. How do you find the right office to call in your telephone book?
4. A form you are filling out uses the word *affidavit*. How could you find out what that word means?
5. Why is it a good idea to fill out forms carefully?
6. What are two places you could read about elections?
7. What should you do if you do not understand election materials?

## Critical Thinking

You are not a citizen of the United States, but you want to become one. How would you use a telephone book to find out how to become a citizen? How would you use a library to study for any tests you might have to take?

## Group Activity

Work with a small group to find information about a political candidate or an important issue facing the country. Look through newspapers and news magazines. Discuss with your group how you would vote based on the information. Then write a group editorial to your local newspaper in which you give your opinion. Be sure to include the reasons for your opinion.

*Money collected from local, state, and federal taxes pays for many different government programs and projects, including road construction and repair.*

# Chapter 17 Paying Taxes

## Words to Know

| | |
|---|---|
| **income tax** | money you need to pay to the government, based on the amount of money you made during the year |
| **withheld** | held back |
| **taxable income** | income that is taxed by the government |
| **dependent** | a person who is supported by another |
| **tax deductions** | costs that can be subtracted from yearly income to help lower taxable income, such as health care costs |
| **itemize** | to list, as tax deductions |
| **extension** | an additional period of time to file taxes |

## Writing Project

Take notes on how to file taxes as you read this chapter. Make sure you put the steps in the correct order. At the end of the chapter, review your notes and write directions about how to file your taxes.

## Learning Objectives

- Find and list key tax information on W-2 and 1099 forms.
- Interpret tax instructions.
- Find information in a tax table.
- Identify places to get tax help.

## SKILL 17.1 Organize Tax Papers

After January 1 of any year, anyone who has earned money in the previous year will start getting important tax information in the mail. The most important information is a W-2 form. A W-2 form helps you figure out the **income tax**, or money you need to pay to the government. It is based on the amount of money you made during the previous year. You will get a W-2 form from each employer you worked for.

Below is a sample W-2 form. It tells what one person earned during the year. This amount is called *Wages, tips, and other compensation.* The W-2 form also tells the taxes that were **withheld**, or held back, from the person's pay during the year. Notice that each box on the W-2 form has a small number or letter in the left corner. These numbers will be useful for filling out tax forms.

| a Control number | Void ☐ | For Official Use Only |
|---|---|---|
| b Employer identification number | 1 Wages, tips, other compensation<br>$4,350.00 | 2 Federal income tax withheld<br>$505.05 |
| c Employer's name, address, and ZIP code<br>Freeman's Medical Supplies<br>1523 River Road<br>Florida City, FL 33034 | 3 Social security wages<br>$4,350.00 | 4 Social security tax withheld<br>$311.07 |
| | 5 Medicare wages and tips | 6 Medicare tax withheld |
| | 7 Social security tips | 8 Allocated tips |
| d Employee's social security number<br>999-00-3534 | 9 Advance EIC payment | 10 Dependent care benefits |
| e Employee's name (first, middle initial, last)<br>Maria Ramirez | 11 Nonqualified plans | 12 Benefits included in box 1 |
| 3123 Rosedale Road<br>Homestead, FL 33032 | 13 See instr. for box 13 | 14 Other |
| f Employee's address and ZIP code | 15 Statutory employee ☐ Deceased ☐ Pension plan ☐ Legal rep. ☐ Deferred compensation ☐ | |

| 16 State Employer's state I.D. no. | 17 State wages, tips, etc. | 18 State income tax | 19 Locality name | 20 Local wages, tips, etc. | 21 Local income tax |
|---|---|---|---|---|---|
| | | $117.24 | | | |

Form **W-2 Wage and Tax Statement 1999** **Copy B** to be filed with employee's federal tax form Dept. of Treasury—IRS

Another important tax form is the 1099. This form lists any taxable interest a person received during the year. For example, interest on savings accounts is considered part of **taxable income.** It must be reported to the Internal Revenue Service (IRS). Here is a sample 1099-INT form (showing interest income).

9292 ☐ VOID ☐ CORRECTED For Official Use Only

| PAYER's name, street address, city, state, and ZIP code | | Payer's RTN (optional) | OMB No. 1545-0012 | |
|---|---|---|---|---|
| Dade County Bank<br>408 Main Street<br>Homestead, FL 33090 | | | **1999**<br>Form **1099-INT** | **Interest Income** |
| PAYER's Federal identification number<br>11-0225611 | RECIPIENT's identification number<br>999-00-3534 | 1 Earnings from savings and loan associations, credit unions, bank deposits, bearer certificates of deposit, etc.<br>$ 193.42 | | **Copy A**<br>**For Internal Revenue Service Center** |
| RECIPIENT's name<br>Maria Ramirez | | 2 Early withdrawal penalty<br>$ | 3 U.S. Savings Bonds, etc.<br>$ | For Privacy Act and Paperwork Reduction Act Notice and instructions for completing this form, see the 1999 instructions for Forms 1099, 1098, 5498, 1096, and W-2G. |
| Street address (including apt. no.)<br>3123 Rosedale Road | | 4 Federal income tax withheld<br>$ | | |
| City, state, and ZIP code<br>Homestead, FL 33032 | | 5 Foreign tax paid (if eligible for foreign tax credit)<br>$ | 6 Foreign country or U.S. possession | |
| Account number (optional) | | | | |

Form **1099-INT** Department of the Treasury – Internal Revenue Service

As you get tax statements, it is up to you to organize them. Here is an example of how you might go about it.

1. Place all the W-2 forms in one envelope or file folder. Label it "W-2."

2. Place all your 1099 forms showing interest in another envelope or file folder. Label it "Interest."

3. If tax forms and instructions come in the mail, place them in a separate envelope or file folder. Label it "Forms and Instructions."

4. File all papers in a safe place.

Do this for all tax statements you receive, and you will have a good start on getting your taxes done.

## Practice

Use a separate sheet of paper to answer these questions.

1. What information is found in Box 1 of the W-2 form on page 206?

2. How much in state taxes was withheld from Maria Ramirez's paycheck in 1999?

3. How much in federal taxes was withheld from Maria Ramirez's paycheck in 1999?

4. Look at Box 1 of the 1099 form on page 207. How much interest did Maria earn in 1999?

5. You are setting up files for your taxes. What three files are you likely to have?

## SKILL 17.2 Complete Tax Forms

Tax forms are worksheets. They help you figure out how much tax you owe. They come with step-by-step instructions. A sample of the 1999 1040EZ tax form is shown on page 209. It is the simplest form you can fill out.

The 1040EZ form is not for everyone. Whether you use it or another kind of tax form, you use the same skills. You read the form. You fill it out carefully and neatly. If you do not understand something, make a note about it. Later, you will get some tips on how to get those questions answered.

Form **1040EZ**

Department of the Treasury—Internal Revenue Service

**Income Tax Return for Single and Joint Filers With No Dependents 1999**

Use the IRS label here.

Your first name and initial | Last name

If a joint return, spouse's first name and initial | Last name

Home address (number and street). | Apt. no.

City, town or post office, state, and ZIP code

Your social security number

Spouse's social security number

▲ IMPORTANT! ▲
You must enter your SSN(s) above.

**Presidential Election Campaign** (See page 12.)

**Note.** *Checking "Yes" will not change your tax or reduce your refund.*

Do you want $3 to go to this fund? ▶ Yes ☐ No ☐

If a joint return, does your spouse want $3 to go to this fund? ▶ Yes ☐ No ☐

Dollars | Cents

## Income

**Attach Copy B of Form(s) W-2 here.** Enclose, but do not staple, any payment.

1 Total wages, salaries, and tips. This should be shown in box 1 of your W-2 form(s). Attach your W-2 form(s). 1

2 Taxable interest. If the total is over $400, you cannot use Form 1040EZ 2

3 Unemployment compensation, qualified state tuition program earnings, and Alaska Permanent Fund dividends (see page 14). 3

4 Add lines 1, 2, and 3. This is your **adjusted gross income.** 4

**Note.** You **must** check Yes or No.

5 Can your parents (or someone else) claim you on their return?
**Yes.** Enter amount from ☐ worksheet on back.
**No.** If **single,** enter 7,050.00. ☐ If **married,** enter 12,700.00. See back for explanation. 5

6 Subtract line 5 from line 4. If line 5 is larger than line 4, enter 0. This is your **taxable income.** ▶ 6

## Payments and tax

7 Enter your Federal income tax withheld from box 2 of your W-2 form(s). 7

8a **Earned income credit** (see page 15).
b Nontaxable earned income: enter type and amount below.
Type | $ 8a

9 Add lines 7 and 8a. These are your **total payments.** 9

10 **Tax.** Use the amount on **line 6 above** to find your tax in the tax table on pages 24–28 of the booklet. Then, enter the tax from the table on this line. 10

## Refund

Have it directly deposited! See page 20 and fill in 11b, 11c, and 11d.

11a If line 9 is larger than line 10, subtract line 10 from line 9. This is your **refund.** 11a

b Routing number ⟶

c Type: Checking ☐ Savings ☐

d Account number ⟶

## Amount you owe

12 If line 10 is larger than line 9, subtract line 9 from line 10. This is the **amount you owe.** See page 21 for details on how to pay. 12

**I have read this return. Under penalties of perjury, I declare that to the best of my knowledge and belief, the return is true, correct, and accurately lists all amounts and sources of income I received during the tax year.**

**Sign here** ▶

Keep copy for your records.

Your signature | Spouse's signature, if joint return

Date | Your occupation | Date | Spouse's occupation

For Official Use Only

1999 Form 1040EZ

## Practice

Use the 1040EZ form on page 209 to answer these questions. Use a separate sheet of paper.

1. On what line do you write the information from Box 1 of your W-2 form?

2. Do you need your social security number to fill out the 1040EZ form?

3. If you are single and no one else can claim you on their tax return, what amount would you enter on line 5?

4. Does giving $3 to the Presidential Election Campaign Fund lower your taxes?

5. What steps on the form help you figure your payments and tax? (Hint: Look at the left column on the form.)

## SKILL 17.3 Read Tax Instructions

**English Tip**
Take the time to think about what you are reading *while* you read it. This will help you learn and remember.

Tax instructions are not just the step-by-step instructions on the front of the form. The 1040EZ form has instructions on the back as well. For example, the instructions on the back of the form tell you that you can use a 1040EZ form if you do not claim any **dependents**, or people who are supported by you. Claiming a dependent is one kind of **tax deduction,** or cost that can be subtracted from your yearly income. It will reduce your tax. Keep track of your deductions by **itemizing**, or listing them. Itemizing your deductions can lower your tax.

The 1040EZ and other tax forms come with a tax instruction booklet. These booklets can be very helpful.

For example, suppose you want to know more about the Presidential Election Campaign Fund. Scan the back of the 1040EZ. You will find the heading *Presidential Election Campaign Fund* and the following explanation.

> This fund helps pay for Presidential election campaigns. The fund reduces candidates' dependence on large contributions from individuals and groups and places candidates on an equal financial footing in the general election.

To make sense of explanations and instructions, you must be skilled in *reading comprehension*. This means that you need to understand what you read. Here is a good way to practice reading comprehension.

1. If you are reading a paragraph, read it one sentence at a time.
2. Read the first sentence slowly to yourself.
3. Ask yourself, "What did I just read?" or "What does this mean I have to do?"
4. If you do not understand the sentence, or do not remember what you just read, read it again.

It is important to file your tax return by the due date. If you cannot, you must file for an **extension**, or an additional period of time to send in your taxes. You can get an extension form at your local tax office.

**Everyday English**

Use your English skills to file a state income tax return, too.

## Practice

Practice your reading comprehension. Read the instructions in the box on page 212. They refer to the 1040EZ form. Then answer the questions that follow on a separate sheet of paper.

*(Practice continues on next page.)* ➪

(Practice continued.)

**Completing Your Return**

Please print your numbers inside the boxes. Do not type your numbers. Do not use dollar signs. You may round off cents to whole dollars. To do so, drop amounts under 50 cents and increase amounts that are 50 cents or more. For example, $129.49 becomes $129 and $129.50 becomes $130. If you round off, do so for all amounts. If you have to add two or more amounts to figure the amount to enter on a line, include cents when adding and round off only the total.

**English and Technology**

You can file your taxes online using IRS *e-file*. The IRS Web site at *www.irs.gov* has information about electronic filing. The Web site also offers tax information.

1. Should you type numbers on your form?
2. Do you have to round off amounts?
3. How would you round off the amount $245.50?
4. How would you round off the amount $998.45?
5. Can you round off some amounts and not others?
6. You have interest from two accounts. One account earned $26.48 in interest. The other earned $31.19 in interest. Line 2 of the 1040EZ form on page 209 asks you to enter the amount of your taxable interest income.

   If you are rounding off all your amounts, which of the following is the correct way to figure your interest?

   **a.** Round off both figures, and then add them.

   **b.** Add them, and then round off the total.

## SKILL 17.4 Use a Tax Table

You are filling out form 1040EZ. Line 10 tells you to find the tax on the amount you entered on line 6. It tells you to use a tax table in the tax booklet.

Whenever you are doing your own taxes, you will have to use a tax table. Here is a small sample from a 1999 tax table.

| **If Form 1040EZ, line 6, is—** | | **And you are—** | |
|---|---|---|---|
| At least | But less than | Single | Married filing jointly |
| | | **Your tax is—** | |
| **4,400** | **4,450** | 664 | 664 |
| **4,450** | **4,500** | 671 | 671 |
| **4,500** | **4,550** | 679 | 679 |
| **4,550** | **4,600** | 686 | 686 |

Line 6 $4543 is in this range.

This column is for filers who are not married.

You use this tax table just as you would any other table. First, you get the amount of your taxable income from your tax form. Your tax form tells you how to do this. Suppose you have filled out the 1040EZ. Your taxable income is $4,543.

Next, you look at the tax table. You locate the range that your taxable income is in. See the first two columns of the tax table on page 213.

Now, run your finger from the range across to the column under the "Single" heading. You can see that the amount of tax you owe is $679.

Read tax tables carefully. Take your time. Always double-check your figures.

## Practice

Use the tax table on page 213. Find the answers to the following questions. Write them on a separate sheet of paper.

1. Your taxable income is $4,425. You are married and filing jointly. How much tax do you owe?

2. Your taxable income is $4,575. You are single. How much tax do you owe?

## SKILL 17.5 Get Help When Needed

You have used all your skills, and you still cannot figure out your taxes. You are not alone. Thousands of people have questions about their tax forms each year. Read the tips on page 215 on getting help.

### Getting Tax Help

1. Your tax booklet has a table of contents and an index. Use them to help you find answers to your questions.

2. Your tax booklet tells you how to locate a toll-free number for the IRS. It also tells you what to do before you call.

3. Libraries often offer free tax help at tax time. Call your library for more information.

4. Private businesses and accountants will do your taxes for a fee. To find them, look under Tax Preparation in the yellow pages.

**Brush Up on the Basics**

Remember to use a comma (,) between the number of the day and the number of the year when writing the date. (See Punctuation 4 in the Reference Guide.)

## Practice

You look in the table of contents of your tax booklet. This is what you see under Section 1.

**Section 1:** Before you fill out your tax return. . . . . . . . . . 5
How do you use this booklet? . . . . . . . . . . . . . . . . . . . . 5
What free tax help is available? . . . . . . . . . . . . . . . . . . 6
What if a taxpayer died? . . . . . . . . . . . . . . . . . . . . . . . . 6
Do you have to file? . . . . . . . . . . . . . . . . . . . . . . . . . . . 8
Which forms should you use? . . . . . . . . . . . . . . . . . . . . 8

**1.** You want to know which forms to use. On which page will you find that information?

**2.** You want to find out how to get help with your taxes. On which page will you find that information?

**3.** You have already filled out your tax form. Is this the section of the book you need? Explain.

Chapter

# 17 Review

## Summary

| |
|---|
| Tax laws and instructions change quite often. English skills can help you handle those changes. |
| Begin by organizing your tax papers. Put them in categories, and then file them. For example, put all W-2s in one file folder and all 1099s in another file folder. |
| Tax instructions are found on the forms and in booklets. Read them slowly and carefully to understand them. |
| Use a tax table to help you figure out the tax you owe. |
| The tax booklet lists places for you to get help on your taxes. Libraries and tax preparation services can also help. |

| |
|---|
| taxable income |
| withheld |
| extension |
| itemize |
| income tax |
| tax deductions |
| dependent |

## Vocabulary Review

**Match each term in the box with its meaning. Write the term and its matching number on a separate sheet of paper.**

1. to list, as tax deductions
2. a person who is supported by another
3. an additional period of time to file taxes
4. income that is taxed by the government
5. money you pay to the government, based on the amount of money you make during the year
6. held back
7. costs that can be subtracted from yearly income to help lower taxable income

## Chapter Quiz

**Answer the following questions in one or two sentences. Use a separate sheet of paper.**

1. What are two skills that can help you file tax forms?
2. What are two pieces of information that can be found on a W-2 form?
3. What tax information do you need from your bank?
4. Josh has the following pieces of information:
   Two W-2 forms; a 1099 on his savings account; a Form 1040EZ; a 1099 on his checking account
   How should he organize them to fill out his tax return?
5. When doing your taxes, can you round off just some of the numbers? Explain.
6. You want to know more about tax deductions. How would you go about looking up deductions in the tax booklet?
7. What is a tax table?
8. What three resources can you use to help you with your taxes?

## Critical Thinking

A friend tells you that you can file your tax forms late by filing for an extension. How would you use your tax booklet to find out how to file for an extension?

### Group Activity

Work with a group to write a scene about someone doing his or her taxes. What information does the person need? Is this person getting a refund? If so, how would he or she react? Make sure your scene has a funny side. Add an unusual problem to solve.

# Unit 5 Review

**Read each sentence below. Then choose the letter that best completes each one.**

1. You can find information for contacting many government agencies
   - A. in a telephone book.
   - B. in fliers sent to taxpayers.
   - C. on your driver's license.
   - D. on your monthly telephone bill.

2. A birth certificate is
   - A. a form for pre-approving a child's birth.
   - B. one kind of proof of residency.
   - C. a form that can always be shown in place of a driver's license.
   - D. an official record containing a person's birth information.

3. Before you can vote in a government election, you must
   - A. have a credit check.
   - B. declare how you plan to vote.
   - C. register to vote.
   - D. give a blood sample.

4. An editorial in a newspaper or on television is
   - A. one source of information about an election issue.
   - B. one group's or person's opinion about an election issue.
   - C. often biased.
   - D. all of the above

5. A W-2 form tells you how much
   - A. money you earned during the year.
   - B. in taxes you owe at the end of the year.
   - C. in taxes you should set aside in the upcoming year.
   - D. money your company earned last year.

6. A tax table
   - A. is set up like a pie chart.
   - B. is the place where you bring your tax payment.
   - C. tells you how much tax you owe based on your income.
   - D. tells you how the government uses your taxes.

**Critical Thinking**

Today, most American adults have the right to vote. However, not all people who can vote go to the polls every election. Do you think more Americans should vote? Explain your answer.

**WRITING** Taxes are a fact of life. Everyone needs to pay them. The government uses the money to pay for roads, the military, and social service programs. On a separate sheet of paper, write an essay describing the pros and cons of paying taxes. Your essay should be at least three paragraphs long.

Unit 6

# English for Health and Safety

Chapter 18
## Getting Health Care

Chapter 19
## Living Safely

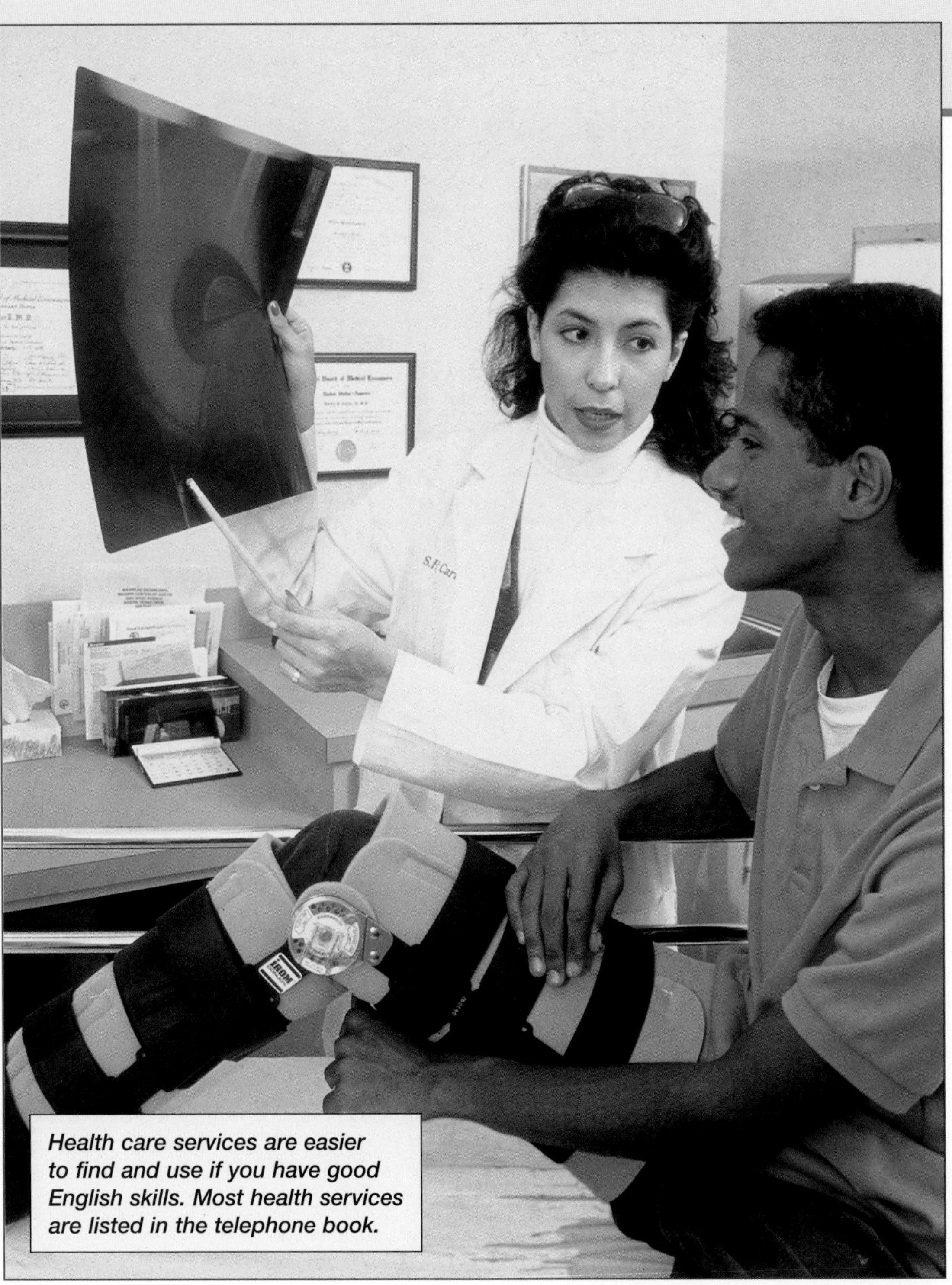

*Health care services are easier to find and use if you have good English skills. Most health services are listed in the telephone book.*

# Chapter 18 Getting Health Care

## Words to Know

| | |
|---|---|
| **Health Maintenance Organization** | a type of company that provides health care insurance |
| **physician** | a medical doctor |
| **psychiatrist** | a medical doctor who specializes in mental health treatment |
| **psychologist** | a professional who specializes in mental health treatment |
| **specialist** | a doctor who treats a particular kind of illness |
| **symptoms** | signs of illness |
| **prescription** | a doctor's order for special medicine |
| **pharmacist** | a person who fills prescriptions |
| **generic** | without a brand name |

### Role-Play Project

Work with a partner to role-play a telephone conversation between a receptionist at a doctor's office and a person who has a sore throat. Write questions the patient should ask. Discuss what the receptionist should do if he or she does not know the answers.

### Learning Objectives

- Identify health care services found in a telephone book.
- Write questions to ask during a health care visit.
- Use a library to learn more about health and health care.
- Explain key information found on medicine labels.

## SKILL 18.1 Use a Phone Book to Find Health Care

Finding good health care is important. The best way is to ask friends, family, and co-workers for recommendations. You can ask what they like about their doctors and dentists.

Many people join a **Health Maintenance Organization (HMO)** through their employer. People in an HMO receive a patient provider list. This is a booklet which lists the doctors in their HMO plan. Patients who visit the doctors in their plan usually save money on their health care costs.

**English Tip**
Your phone book probably has an index to the yellow pages. Use it to help find the health care services you need.

A phone book or patient provider list shows many kinds of health care professionals. The following chart explains some of the most common headings.

| If You Need | Look Under |
|---|---|
| Health care | **"Physicians"** in the yellow pages or in a patient provider list |
| Tooth care | "Dentists" in the yellow pages or in a patient provider list |
| Help dealing with problems, bad thoughts, feelings, or behavior | "Mental Health Services," **"Psychiatrists,"** or **"Psychologists"** in the yellow pages or in a patient provider list |
| Special problems, such as drinking too much | The area of treatment, such as "Alcoholism" in the yellow pages |
| Help paying for treatment | "City or County Health Services" in the Government Listings of the white pages |

## Practice

Use the chart on page 222 to answer the following questions. Write your answers on a separate sheet of paper.

1. Jennifer has a sore throat that is getting worse. What heading should she look under to get treatment?

2. Ibrahim cannot afford to pay for medical treatment. Where can he look for help?

3. Matt needs to have his teeth cleaned. How can he find a health care professional to do the job?

4. Tula has been feeling sad and lonely for a long time. She thinks she needs professional help. How could she find it in a phone book?

## SKILL 18.2 Find Specialists

Sometimes you need a **specialist**, a doctor who treats only one kind of condition. In the yellow pages, there is often a section that groups doctors by type of practice. If you belong to an HMO, your regular doctor will give you a referral to see a particular specialist.

### Everyday English

Do you have the phone number of your doctor with you at all times? If not, where could you carry it?

**Brush Up on the Basics**

Remember that you do not use a capital letter with a title or position that is not used before a person's name. For example, Matt is a *doctor*. (See Capitalization 4 in the Reference Guide.)

This special section in the yellow pages is sometimes called "Physicians and Surgeons Guide." In this section you will find headings for specialties such as the ones below.

- **Family and General Practice**
  Includes doctors who treat most kinds of common illnesses
- **Dermatology**
  Includes doctors who specialize in skin care
- **Pediatrics**
  Includes doctors who specialize in treating infants and children

When you need special health care, look through this yellow pages section. You might find a doctor to suit your needs.

## Practice

Read the information from the yellow pages on the next page. Then answer the questions below.

1. You have aching joints. A friend says you might have arthritis. You look up "Arthritis" in the yellow pages. What does it tell you to do?
2. Where could you go for acne treatment?
3. What kinds of care do plastic surgeons offer?
4. Michelle Dern is your family doctor. Under which heading would you find her number?

## Physicians & Surgeons Guide

**ARTHRITIS**

SEE *Rheumatology*

**DERMATOLOGY**

**Mark Bonner MD**
3099 E. 13th St., Oaklyn . . . . . . . . . . . . . . . . . 555-0098

**Dora Chui MD**

**Skin Cancer • Moles • Acne**
Located near Market & 5th St., Oaklyn . . . 555-3247
674 5th St., Camden . . . . . . . . . . . . . . . . . 555-9876

**Patrick Donnely MD**
9908 Potter Rd., Camden . . . . . . . . . . . . . . . . 555-0987

**FAMILY AND GENERAL PRACTICE**

**Michelle Dern MD**
1212 Walnut St., Oaklyn . . . . . . . . . . . . . . . . . 555-0433

**PLASTIC AND RECONSTRUCTIVE SURGERY**

**Nina Gonzalez MD**

10143 Franklin Blvd., Kent . . . . . . . . . . . . 555-3053
*Certified by American Board of Plastic Surgeons*

- Neck and Face Lifts
- Scar Revision
- Dermabrasion

**Everyday English**

Could you use a dictionary to find out what a podiatrist does? Try it and find out.

### English and Technology

Some Web sites offer health care information online. These Web sites can help you understand your health care options.

**Tips for Making Doctors' Appointments**

When you make an appointment, be prepared. Here are some tips.

1. Give your name and **symptoms**, or signs of illness. Make sure the doctor can treat your problem.

2. If the doctor cannot help you, ask for the name of someone who can.

3. Ask about charges and payment. If you have a health plan, make sure the doctor will accept it.

4. Have paper, a pencil, and a calendar handy. Write down the appointment date and time.

## SKILL 18.3 Take Part in Your Own Health Care

The year was 1542. John Thomas went to his doctor. John had been having terrible headaches. "Well, we'll just have to bleed you," said the doctor to John.

John let the doctor cut his arm open, and John never questioned his doctor about this treatment. "After all," John thought, "doctors know a lot more than I do."

These days, many doctors believe that patients get well more quickly if they take part in their own health care. Your English skills can help you do this. First, it is good to write down a list of questions for your health care professional. Why should you write them down? Doctors are often busy and in a hurry. You may be nervous and forgetful during the office visit. A written list of questions will help you and the doctor. Here are some questions you might ask.

1. Are there any treatments other than the one you are recommending?

2. Does this medicine have any side effects I should know about?

3. What can I do to prevent getting sick again?

You can also read about health. Your library has many books on health care. There are "self-help" books on how to look and feel better. An encyclopedia can tell you about many diseases and their causes. A library's card catalog and reference room are important tools for finding out about health care. You can also search the Internet for Web sites dealing with health.

## Practice

Use a separate sheet of paper to write the answers to the following questions.

**1.** Your dermatologist wants to remove a mole on your arm. He says it looks "suspicious." What are three questions you would ask?

**2.** Your knee aches. You want to read about possible causes and treatments *before* you see a doctor. How would you use a library to help you?

**3.** You have a bad cough. Your doctor writes an order for special medicine for you. What are three questions you would ask your doctor?

## SKILL 18.4 Read Medicine Labels Carefully

Amanda found a doctor in the yellow pages. The doctor checked her symptoms and said she had strep throat. Amanda went to a pharmacy and picked up a **prescription**, or doctor's order for special medication, from a **pharmacist**, or person who fills prescriptions. She then read the label carefully before taking the medicine.

All medicine labels contain important information. They tell you how much and how often to take a medicine. Here is some other important information found on labels.

- The medicine's name
- The number of refills you can get
- The number of pills in the bottle

Here is an example of a prescription medicine label and information about how to read it.

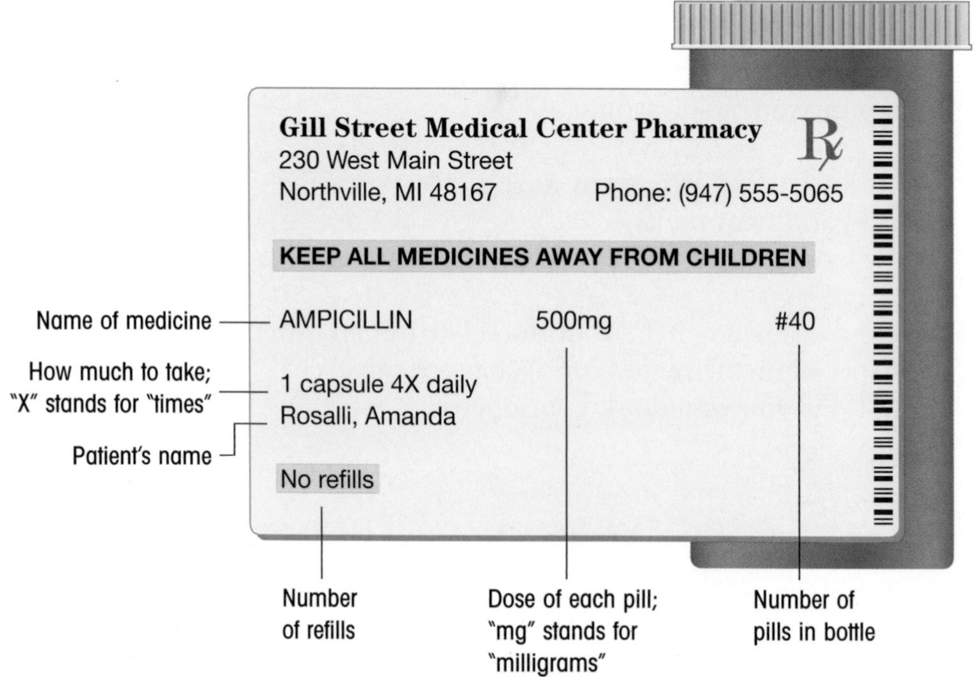

Look for the word **generic** on medicine labels. Generic drugs do not have brand names. They are usually less expensive than those with brand names.

## Practice

Answer the following questions using the prescription label on page 228.

1. What does #40 mean?
2. How many refills can Amanda get?
3. What does *mg* stand for?
4. How many pills should Amanda take per day?
5. What is the name of the medicine Amanda is taking?
6. Where did Amanda have the prescription filled?
7. What warning is on the prescription label?
8. What is the patient's full name?
9. What is the address of the pharmacy?
10. Whose phone number is on the label?

Chapter

# 18 Review

## Summary

| |
|---|
| Find health care services by asking friends and family. Also use a telephone book. |
| Look under different telephone book headings and look over telephone listings to find special services. |
| Write down questions to ask your health care specialist. |
| Use a library to learn more about health care and prevention of illness. |
| Read key information on medicine labels for safety. |

| |
|---|
| pharmacist |
| generic |
| symptoms |
| psychologist |
| prescription |
| psychiatrist |
| specialist |
| physician |
| Health Maintenance Organization |

## Vocabulary Review

**Complete each sentence below with a term from the box. Use a separate sheet of paper.**

1. Another word for medical doctor is ____.
2. The label on a ____ should be read carefully.
3. Someone who fills prescriptions is called a ____.
4. A ____ is a doctor who treats only one kind of condition.
5. When you make a doctor's appointment, always give your name and the ____ you are having.
6. A ____ is a professional who specializes in mental health treatment.
7. A medicine that does not have a brand name is usually labeled ____.
8. A company that provides health care insurance is a ____.
9. A medical doctor who specializes in mental health treatment is called a ____.

## Chapter Quiz

**Answer the following questions in one or two sentences. Use a separate sheet of paper.**

**1.** What are two ways to find health care services?

**2.** You want dental advice. How do you use a phone book to get it?

**3.** What section of a phone book can help you find specialists? Give an example of a specialist.

**4.** What should you have next to the phone when you are making a doctor's appointment?

**5.** Why should you write down questions before you see a doctor?

**6.** Why should you bother reading a medicine label?

**7.** You read this on a medicine label: *2 pills 3x daily after meals*. What does it mean?

## Critical Thinking

Choose one of the following health care topics. Write three questions you have about the topic. Then write two ways you could get those questions answered.

**1.** AIDS

**2.** bone marrow transplants

**3.** chicken pox

**4.** hepatitis

## Group Activity

Work with a group to discuss what advice you could give to someone who has hurt his or her shoulder but does not have a doctor. Be sure to include information on how to find medical care and how to use a library for medical research. Share your information with the class.

A quick, organized response is important in an emergency. Keeping an emergency aid by the telephone can save time and maybe even someone's life.

# Chapter 19 Living Safely

## Words to Know

| | |
|---|---|
| **crisis hotline** | an emergency telephone number to call in a serious situation |
| **antidote** | a treatment for poisoning |
| **external** | outside |
| **internal** | inside |
| **hazard** | a danger |

### Emergency Aid Project

Your parents have asked you to watch your baby brother while they go out. What do you know about keeping him safe? What information do you need to keep your brother safe? Write a list of ten questions to ask your parents before they leave.

### Learning Objectives

- Identify and list emergency numbers found in a telephone book.
- Write an emergency aid for home use.
- Recognize ten "survival" words.
- Interpret safety information, warnings, and first aid instructions on labels.

## SKILL 19.1 Write an Emergency Aid

In an emergency, it is important to act fast and stay calm. A telephone is often your most important tool.

Most communities have a 911 emergency number. You can call this number for any life-threatening emergency. This includes fires, crimes, and accidental poisoning. If your community does not have 911 service, look in the front of the white pages. You will find police and fire emergency numbers listed there. You will also find **crisis hotline** numbers.

One example of a crisis hotline number is the poison control center. Anyone can call this number and get advice on poisons and their **antidotes**, or treatments.

Even looking in a phone book can take time. So it is a good idea to make an emergency aid for your home. An emergency aid should include phone numbers for

- police department, fire department, and poison control center.
- helpful neighbors.
- children's doctor and medical insurance information.
- relatives to call in case of emergency.

Keep the emergency aid by the main phone. On the next page is one person's emergency aid, set up in chart form.

**Everyday English**

Where is the best place to keep an emergency aid in your home?

| In an emergency, call | Phone Number | Address |
|---|---|---|
| Police | 911 | |
| Fire Department | 911 | |
| Poison Control | 555-3348 | |
| Dr. Lubblow | 555-8760 | 777 Oscar Street, Oakland |
| Tom Parker (neighbor) | 555-8855 | 980 13th Street, Apt. 6 |
| Elsie June (neighbor) | 555-7120 | 975 13th Street |
| Nancy Lee (grandmother) | 555-9875 | 440 Green Street, Emeryville |
| | | |
| Kid's HealthShield Medical Insurance Numbers: | | |
| Sara Ann Lee | 8903-90002 | |
| Harry Lee | 7892-00934 | |

## Practice

Write your own home emergency aid on a separate sheet of paper. Use the white pages to find emergency phone numbers. Include at least one family member or neighbor who should be called in case of emergency.

## SKILL 19.2 Interpret Words That Mean Danger

**Everyday English**

What other kinds of emergency aids could you write for your home?

You can keep many emergencies from ever happening. How? By reading and paying attention to the words around you.

Here are ten important words or phrases you should know. When you see one of them, take note. It could save your life or someone else's.

| Ten Survival Words and Phrases for Safety | |
|---|---|
| 1. **Combustible**<br>2. **Flammable**<br>3. **Inflammable** | Nearby heat or fire could cause an explosion. |
| 4. **For External Use Only** | Use this only on the outside of the body. |
| 5. **Not For Internal Use** | Do not put this inside the body. |
| 6. **Noxious** | This is harmful to health in some way. |
| 7. **Contaminated** | This is poisoned or polluted. |
| 8. **Condemned** | This sign is usually seen on a building. It means the building is unlivable or dangerous and must be torn down. |
| 9. **Prohibited** | Stay away from or do not use. |
| 10. **Do Not Inhale Fumes** | Do not breathe near this product or site. |

## Practice

Use a separate sheet of paper to answer these questions.

1. A spray can is labeled *Inflammable.* Where should you store it?

2. A building is labeled *Condemned.* What does that mean?

3. A sign in front of a river says *Contaminated.* Should you swim in the river? Explain.

4. What does *Noxious* mean?

5. A bottle is labeled *For **external,** or outside, use only. Not for **internal,** or inside, use.* What should you do if a child drinks from the bottle? Why?

## SKILL 19.3 Read Safety Information

In Chapter 17, you practiced your reading comprehension skills. Use those same skills when you read product labels and safety instructions. Remember to read one sentence at a time slowly. Then ask yourself, "What does that mean to me?" before you go on. On the next page are some everyday situations where you will need to read safety information.

**Brush Up on the Basics**

When reading warning labels, pay special attention to the adverb *not*. *Not* changes the meaning of a verb or verb phrase in a subject. (See Grammar 42 in the Reference Guide.)

> **Everyday English**
>
> Do you know much about first aid? Use your English skills to look up the nearest Red Cross chapter. The Red Cross offers first aid classes all the time. You can also get books on safety and first aid from your library.

- When using household products and taking medicines, always read the labels first.
- When doing repairs, read about safety **hazards,** or dangers, and special procedures in manuals. If you are working near electricity, call a professional for help.
- If there is a child in the house, get a book from a library on home safety. It will give you tips on covering up light sockets, locking cupboards, and more.

## Practice

Read the label below. Then use a separate sheet of paper to answer the questions on the next page.

**BRITE WHITE**
**BLEACH**

**IMPORTANT: DO NOT MIX WITH ANY HOUSEHOLD CLEANING AGENT EXCEPT SOAPS AND DETERGENTS. MIXING MAY PRODUCE NOXIOUS FUMES.**

**WARNING:** Do not get on skin or eyes. If splashed on skin or eyes, flood with water for 15 minutes. Call a doctor.

If taken internally, give milk or bread soaked in milk, followed by cooking oil. Call a doctor immediately.

1. With what can you mix the bleach?

2. What are noxious fumes?

3. What should you do if the bleach gets in your eyes?

4. Should you wear rubber gloves when you use this bleach? Explain why or why not.

5. What should you do if a child drinks the bleach?

6. Where should you store this bleach?

7. Can you add this bleach to a laundry detergent?

8. What is one emergency phone number you should keep near the bleach?

9. What information should you be ready to give when you call an emergency number?

### English and Careers

Some jobs involve being around cleaning supplies and other strong chemicals. Workers at these jobs must read and understand many safety warnings.

# Chapter 19 Review

## Summary

Emergency numbers can often be found in the front of the white pages.

An emergency aid by the telephone can save valuable time. An aid should include names and telephone numbers of agencies, neighbors, doctors, and relatives.

To prevent emergencies, pay attention and read carefully. Safety information can be found on household products, in manuals, and in books.

| antidote |
|---|
| crisis hotline |
| internal |
| external |
| hazard |

## Vocabulary Review

**Match each term in the box with its meaning. Write the term and its matching number on a separate sheet of paper.**

**1.** a danger

**2.** outside

**3.** inside

**4.** an emergency phone number

**5.** a treatment for poisoning

## Chapter Quiz

**Answer the following questions in one or two sentences. Use a separate sheet of paper.**

1. Where can you find emergency phone numbers?
2. Why is it a good idea to have an emergency aid by the phone?
3. What are three things that should be included on an emergency aid?
4. What should you have in front of you when you call a poison control center? Why?
5. What does *combustible* mean?
6. What does it mean if something is *prohibited*?
7. Why should you read labels on household products before using them?
8. What should you do before you use a power saw for the first time?

## Critical Thinking

In Chapter 11, you wrote step-by-step job aids for work. You can write step-by-step aids for emergencies in your home, too.

Use a library's card catalog or the Internet to find information about hurricane safety. Then write a step-by-step emergency aid for a family that lives in hurricane territory. Use a separate sheet of paper.

## Group Activity

Work with a group to discuss some everyday safety hazards and how you can protect yourself. Then design a poster to warn other students in your school about the safety hazards.

# Unit 6 Review

**Read each sentence below. Then choose the letter that best completes each one.**

**1.** A fever, a runny nose, and an aching throat are all examples of

- **A.** referrals.
- **B.** symptoms.
- **C.** generics.
- **D.** prescriptions.

**2.** You would most likely find a yellow page listing for psychiatrists under the heading

- **A.** "Clinics."
- **B.** "Pharmacies."
- **C.** "Mental Health Services."
- **D.** "Dentists."

**3.** A dermatologist is a doctor who treats

- **A.** skin diseases.
- **B.** ear, nose, and throat diseases.
- **C.** lung diseases.
- **D.** mental health diseases.

**4.** All of the following pieces of information appear on a medicine label, except

- **A.** the name of your illness.
- **B.** the number of refills you can get.
- **C.** how often to take the drug.
- **D.** the medicine's name.

**5.** A good place to keep an emergency aid is

- **A.** next to the telephone.
- **B.** in a file cabinet.
- **C.** in a kitchen drawer.
- **D.** near the front door.

**6.** If a medicine is labeled "For External Use Only," then you should never

- **A.** touch it.
- **B.** drink it.
- **C.** rub it on your hands.
- **D.** spray it on your skin.

**7.** A condemned building is

- **A.** ready to be torn down.
- **B.** not livable.
- **C.** very dangerous.
- **D.** all of the above

**Critical Thinking**

Why is it important to have a plan of action in place before an emergency happens?

**WRITING** Many people believe that health care is a partnership between a patient and a doctor. On a separate sheet of paper, write an essay in which you explain why it is important for you to have a role in your own health care. Describe at least three ways that you can take part in your health care. Your essay should be at least three paragraphs long.

Unit 7

# English for Recreation

Chapter 20
## Reading Newspapers and Magazines

Chapter 21
## Traveling, Eating Out, and Cooking

*Newspapers and magazines give you a lot of information for very little money. Using the index can help you quickly find the sections you want to read first.*

# Chapter 20 Reading Newspapers and Magazines

## Words to Know

| | |
|---|---|
| **headlines** | titles of newspaper or magazine articles |
| **current events** | things that are happening now |
| **subscribe** | to order |
| **subscription** | a form for ordering a magazine or newspaper |

### News Project

Look through newspapers to find a news article that interests you. Read the article. Then takes notes on the article. Use your notes to write a short paragraph summarizing the article.

### Learning Objectives

- Use the index and headlines to find articles and features in newspapers.
- Explain the difference between hard news and soft news.
- Find key information in news articles.
- Identify three places to find magazines.
- Fill out a magazine subscription card.

## SKILL 20.1 Find What You Want

**Brush Up on the Basics**

When reading a newspaper article, be sure you know which noun a pronoun such as *he* or *she* is referring to. (See Grammar 27 in the Reference Guide.)

Have you ever wanted to know what movies are playing over the weekend? Would you like to know if your favorite team won the game last night? Are you interested in learning more about events in your neighborhood? In your state? All over the world?

You can find all of this information and more in a newspaper. Newspapers print articles about politics, sports, concerts, local issues, and even cooking. All this and more can be yours for less than a dollar a day.

Not everyone reads the entire newspaper. Most people read only what interests them. Most people use **headlines**, or the titles of articles, to help them find what they want. Headlines have key words that tell what an article is about.

### Practice

Use a separate sheet of paper to answer these questions.

**1.** What do you think you would find in an article with each headline?

- a. Space Probe Finds No Life On Mars
- b. Top Singer to Perform Free in Park
- c. President Speaks To Nation On Air Pollution
- d. Happenings About Town

**2.** Of the four headlines, which interests you the most? Why?

## SKILL 20.2 Use a Newspaper Index

In addition to headlines, you can use a newspaper's index to help you find areas of interest. The index is usually placed at the bottom of the first page of a newspaper. Look at the following index.

**Inside**

| | | | |
|---|---|---|---|
| Autos | C17 | Horoscope | B6 |
| Books | E5 | Letters | A24 |
| Bridge | B7 | Movies | E4 |
| Business | C1 | Obituaries | B5 |
| Chess | B7 | People | B3 |
| Classified | B8 | Radio | E6 |
| Comics | B9 | Sports | D1 |
| Crossword | A25 | TV | E6 |
| Editorials | A24 | Theater | E2 |
| Events | E1 | Weather | C6 |

Notice that different types of articles and features are listed in alphabetical order. The letter-number combination following each listing tells you

- the section of the newspaper in which you will find the article or feature. (The first section of a newspaper is always called "A.")
- the page number on which to look.

For example, suppose you want to look at the "Want Ads" in the Classified listings. The Classifieds are in section B on page 8.

**English and Technology**

Many newspapers are available on the Internet. Often, you can e-mail a letter to the editor to express your opinion.

## Practice

Use a separate sheet of paper to answer these questions about the index on page 247.

1. Where will you find the movie listings?
2. You are thinking about buying a new car. What section has articles that would interest you?
3. Does this newspaper have a crossword puzzle?
4. Where would you find book reviews?
5. Where would you look to find out if your favorite baseball team won or lost last night?

## SKILL 20.3 Read the News

**Everyday English**

What are the names of the local newspapers in your area? How much do they cost?

You will find most of the "hard news" stories in the first section of a newspaper. Hard news stories describe important **current events**, or things that are happening in the world now. A hard news story may be about a tornado or an important meeting between two world leaders.

"Soft news" stories are meant to entertain as well as inform you. One soft news story told of a family visit to a folk music museum. Other soft news stories focus on local plays, movies, people, and events.

In both hard and soft news stories, the most important facts are in the first part of the article. Most news writers try to answer the *who, what, why, where, when,* and *how* questions in the first few paragraphs. That way, readers can get the most important information quickly and easily. If the article interests you, you can read further.

## Practice

Read the following news story. Then use a separate sheet of paper to answer the questions.

**WAREHOUSE EXPLODES! THREE ESCAPE**

RICHMOND (April 17)—A Richmond warehouse filled with paint exploded at 11:15 P.M. last night. Three workers escaped without injury. The warehouse, located at Fifth and Tennessee Streets, caught on fire at approximately 10:30 P.M. Heat from the fire caused 5,000 gallons of paint to explode and blast the roof off the building. Firefighters controlled the blaze by 2 A.M. this morning.

A night security officer and two workers escaped the burning building before the explosion. All are in good condition. No other injuries were reported. Fire officials do not know the cause of the fire at this time.

"I'm glad I wasn't in there when it blew," said security guard Rocky Brookens. "It felt as if a bomb had gone off. I'm lucky to be alive."

**English Tip**
The most important information always comes at the beginning of a news article.

1. What is this story about?
2. Where did the fire occur?
3. Who was on hand at the fire scene?
4. When did it happen?
5. Why did it happen?
6. Is this a hard news story or soft news story? Why?

## SKILL 20.4 Use Magazines

Magazines are a great resource for many things. Crafts magazines can help you learn how to make models, sew, build gliders, and more. There are magazines to keep you fit and help you get a job. News magazines cover current events in more detail than newspapers.

The best place to find a magazine that interests you is a library. You can browse through the magazine area or periodical room to find interesting magazines. You can use the *Readers' Guide to Periodical Literature* to find articles that interest you. Many stores and newsstands have magazine racks, too. Even a doctor's waiting room is well-stocked with magazines to fill the time until the doctor sees you.

When you pick out a magazine, scan the table of contents. This important skill will help you find articles that interest you most.

### Practice

The following table of contents is from a news magazine. Look it over. Then answer the questions on page 251 on a separate sheet of paper.

WORLD EVENTS: Russian-U.S. Relations Today . . . . . . . 12
NATIONAL EVENTS: New Life for Old Cities . . . . . . . . . 36
HEALTH: New Hope for Bald Heads . . . . . . . . . . . . . . . 51
EDUCATION: Computers in Schools . . . . . . . . . . . . . . . 62
SPORTS: Home Run King Strikes Out . . . . . . . . . . . . . . 79
LAW: Justice and the Teenager . . . . . . . . . . . . . . . . . . 98
TRAVEL: The Ten Best Vacation Getaways . . . . . . . . . . 109

1. Daryl is planning a vacation in August. Can this magazine help him? If so, how?

2. Carlos has noticed that his hairline is not what it used to be. Is there anything in this magazine for him? If so, what?

3. Suzanne has to do a report for school on an international issue. What section in this magazine would give her some ideas?

## SKILL 20.5 Subscribe to a Magazine

A magazine may have only one or two articles of interest to you. However, if you are a true sports fan, you may want to read anything and everything about sports. You might want to **subscribe** to, or order, a sports magazine. If you subscribe, the magazine will come right to your home. Often, the cost per magazine is less when you subscribe.

The easiest way to subscribe is to buy a copy of the magazine. Inside you will usually find a form for ordering a magazine or newspaper, or a **subscription** card. Look for this key information on the card.

- The price of the subscription
- The time periods for which you can subscribe
- The way to pay for the magazine

When you know what you want, fill in the card. Then enjoy your magazine!

**Everyday English**

Is there a magazine that you especially like? What makes it enjoyable to you?

## Practice

Below is a sample subscription card. Look it over. Then answer the questions on the next page, on a separate sheet of paper.

# Celebrity View Magazine

Last Name First Name Middle Initial

Street No. Apt. No.

City State Zip Code

**SAVE $2.00 AN ISSUE OFF THE NEWSSTAND PRICE. HAVE CELEBRITY VIEW DELIVERED RIGHT TO YOUR OWN HOME.**

Check one:

____ I want 12 issues (one year) for $19.95

____ I want 24 issues (two years) for $37.95

____ I want 36 issues (three years) for $54.95

Check your method of payment:

____ Check or money order enclosed.

Credit Card Number Expiration Date

____ Bill me later.

HOLLYWOOD

Now Showing

1. For what time periods can you subscribe?

2. How much money would you save if you subscribed for one year rather than buy 12 different issues at a newstand?

3. You want to pay for the subscription now. Do you have this choice? Explain.

Suppose you have subscribed to CELEBRITY VIEW magazine. What makes this the perfect magazine for you? Use your imagination to answer the following questions.

4. What type of magazine is this?

5. What are some articles that might appear in this magazine? Create a table of contents making up at least six titles for articles you would like to read.

6. Who or what would have to be on the cover of this magazine for you to buy it at a store?

# Chapter 20 Review

## Summary

Reading newspapers and magazines is a way to stay in touch with the world around you. You can use them to learn about current events, sports, hobbies, and entertainment.

Newspapers contain many features and articles. Some are soft news, and others are hard news. Headlines and the index help you to find the articles that interest you most.

News articles answer the *who, what, why, where, when,* and *how* questions. Usually, the most important information is in the first few paragraphs.

Magazines on many subjects can be found in a library and on newsstands. You can use the table of contents to find the articles that interest you most. Subscribing to a magazine can save you money and time.

| headlines |
| --- |
| current events |
| subscribe |
| subscription |

## Vocabulary Review

**Match each term in the box with its meaning. Write the term and its matching number on a separate sheet of paper.**

1. form for ordering a magazine
2. titles of newspaper articles
3. to order
4. things that are happening now

## Chapter Quiz

**Answer the following questions in one or two sentences. Use a separate sheet of paper.**

1. What are two reasons to read a newspaper?
2. What are two ways that you could find entertainment information in newspapers?
3. How can reading headlines save you time?
4. What are three types of articles or features that might be listed in the newspaper index?
5. An index lists the Comics on E-15. What does that mean?
6. What are two examples of a hard news story?
7. What are two examples of a soft news story?
8. How are hard and soft news stories different?
9. What are three places where you could find magazines?
10. Why would you subscribe to a magazine?

## Critical Thinking

In the next two days, take notes on an event that happens around you. It can be soft news or hard news. Then write a short article about it. Answer the *who, what, why, where, when,* and *how* questions in the first two paragraphs.

### Group Activity

Work with a partner to write a short story about a world without newspapers. What would be different? How would information be passed along? Would businesses suffer? Would the world become a better place?

*Practical English skills have a place in recreation as well as at work. When you are planning a trip, you need to understand what you read.*

Chapter 21

# Traveling, Eating Out, and Cooking

## Words to Know

| | |
|---|---|
| **entree** | a main course |
| **a la carte** | a separate price for each item on a menu |
| **recipe** | a set of directions for preparing food |
| **ingredients** | what a prepared food contains |
| **brochures** | booklets |
| **toll free** | without a charge |
| **reservations** | arrangements to save a place |
| **agenda** | a list of things to do |

## Recipe Project

On an index card, write a recipe for your favorite food. On one side of the index card, list all of the ingredients needed to prepare the dish. Use abbreviations. On the other side of the index card, list the steps you need to follow to make the recipe. Exchange recipes with a partner.

## Learning Objectives

- Interpret words in context.
- Identify abbreviations and follow directions in recipes.
- Identify three resources to use for planning trips.
- Compare travel information.

## SKILL 21.1 Figure Out What Words Mean

Sean is reading a restaurant review in the food section of his newspaper. The review says, "The entrees, especially the lemon swordfish, are wonderful." Sean does not know what *entree* means. Since he is at home, he could look up *entree* in the dictionary. Suppose he is not at home. He could figure out the meaning of the word by

- studying how it is used in the sentence.
- using his own experience.
- making an "educated guess."

**Here is an example.**

Sean reads the sentence, *The entrees, especially the lemon swordfish, are wonderful.*

> He knows that lemon swordfish is a food, so he knows that the word entree has something to do with food.
>
> He has had fish at restaurants before, always for the main course.

He decides that **entrees** are probably main courses.

This time, Sean is right. He may not always be right, but this skill of making educated guesses is very useful for figuring out new words. Take a look at the menu on page 259. Then make your own educated guesses about what some of the words mean.

**Everyday English**

Some people are embarrassed to ask the meanings of words on a menu. Should they be?

## Practice

Use the menu below to answer the questions on page 260. Write your answers on a separate sheet of paper.

Welcome to

Today's Menu

**Appetizers**

green salad . . . . . . . . . . . . . . . . . . . . . . . . . . . . . . . 3.95
Ma's chicken soup . . . . . . . . . . . . . . . . . . . . . . . . . 2.95
fresh raw vegetables . . . . . . . . . . . . . . . . . . . . . . . 4.95

**Entrees**

meat loaf . . . . . . . . . . . . . . . . . . . . . . . . . . . . . . . . . 7.95
fried chicken . . . . . . . . . . . . . . . . . . . . . . . . . . . . . 6.95
red snapper . . . . . . . . . . . . . . . . . . . . . . . . . . . . . . 8.95
hamburger . . . . . . . . . . . . . . . . . . . . . . . . . . . . . . . 5.95

(All entrees served with choice of potato and soup or salad, or a la carte for $1.00 less.)

**Desserts**

Ma's apple pie . . . . . . . . . . . . . . . . . . . . . . . . . . . . 2.95
ice cream . . . . . . . . . . . . . . . . . . . . . . . . . . . . . . . . 2.45
cheesecake . . . . . . . . . . . . . . . . . . . . . . . . . . . . . . . 3.95

**Today's *prix fixe* meal:**
fresh green salad, grilled fish, steamed vegetables, baked potato, and Ma's apple pie
Only $10.95

*(Practice continues on next page.)* ➪

(Practice continued.)

1. Look at the word *appetizers*. Which of the following do you think has the same meaning?

   **a.** sweets  **b.** starters  **c.** main course

   Write down one clue you got from the menu that helped you make your choice.

> **English Tip**
> Menus often include words from other languages, such as a la carte. Use the context to figure out the meaning of these words.

2. Find the sentence with the French phrase **a la carte**. Which of the following do you think has the same meaning?

   **a.** charged separately, without potato and soup or salad

   **b.** served on a cart

   **c.** baked instead of fried

   Write down one clue in the sentence that helped you make your choice.

3. Find the French words *prix fixe* (pronounced prēē fēēks) on the menu. Which of the following do you think has the same meaning?

   **a.** fresh fish

   **b.** fixed price

   **c.** free food

   Write down one clue that helped you make your choice.

## SKILL 21.2 Use a Cookbook

You have decided to have friends come over for dinner. For ideas about what to serve, you pull out a cookbook.

You can use many of the skills you have already practiced to find a good **recipe**, or directions for preparing food. Suppose you are looking for a tasty dessert. You look in the table of contents and find a whole chapter on desserts. Individual recipes are also listed in the index. So if you know you want to make banana bread, just look in the index under *bananas* or *bread*. Chances are good that you will find the page number for a banana bread recipe.

**Brush Up on the Basics**

Many recipes use fractions. If you are writing out a recipe for a friend, be sure to use hyphens in any fractions you spell out. (See Punctuation 23 in the Reference Guide.)

Once you find a recipe, you will see a list of **ingredients**, or what a prepared food contains. Here is an example.

### Quick Banana Bread

- 1 lb mashed bananas
- $\frac{3}{4}$ c sugar
- 1 egg
- 4 T butter, melted and cooled
- $1\frac{1}{2}$ c flour
- 1 t salt
- 1 t baking soda
- $\frac{1}{2}$ c nuts, chopped

The abbreviations *lb, c, t,* and *T* refer to amounts. Use the chart below to help you learn what they stand for.

| | |
|---|---|
| lb | pound |
| oz | ounce |
| tsp or t | teaspoon |
| tbl or T | tablespoon |
| c | cup |
| qt | quart |
| min | minute |
| hr | hour |

## Practice

On a separate sheet of paper, write the ingredients for quick banana bread. Do not use abbreviations.

## SKILL 21.3 Follow the Directions

**English and Careers**

Many professional chefs use English skills to plan dishes, record recipes, and make job aids for their cooking staffs.

Recipes are simply directions. They tell you what to do. Read through the directions of a recipe twice before you begin. Make sure you are prepared. Then complete the steps, one by one. If the recipe is good, your food will be good, too.

## Practice

Read the recipe directions below. Then answer the questions on a separate sheet of paper.

**Quick Banana Bread**

Preheat oven to 325°. Lightly grease and flour a 9" X 5" loaf pan. Mash bananas in a bowl. Beat in sugar, egg, and butter. In another bowl mix flour, salt, and baking soda. Combine ingredients from both bowls. Add the nuts. Pour into pan and bake for 1 hour.

1. What size pan should you use?
2. How many bowls do you need?
3. What do you think *preheat* means?
4. About how much time will it take to make this bread, including preparation time?

## SKILL 21.4 Plan a Trip

You want to plan a short trip. You can talk to people about places they have visited and liked. You can do some reading on your own.

There are many places to read about traveling. Here are some of the best places to look.

- The travel section of a newspaper
- Guidebooks found in libraries or bookstores
- **Brochures**, or booklets, from travel agents or auto clubs
- Travel magazines
- Internet sites about travel

All of these resources can help you decide on the right trip. As you read, you will want to take notes and make some comparisons. What are the costs? What sights can you see? Is it a city trip or country trip? How will you travel?

These resources might also list ways you can get more information. Perhaps they will contain a **toll free** number, a telephone number without a charge. What should you do when you know where you want to go? Make **reservations**, or arrangements to save a place. You can make reservations by phone, on the Internet, or through a travel agent. Travel agents will make reservations for you and help you plan a trip at no cost.

**Everyday English**

How could you use a telephone book to find a travel agent?

## Practice

Use a separate sheet of paper to complete the following activities.

1. Explain how you would find guidebooks on Colorado in a library.

2. Read the following passages from a guidebook.

> Hot Springs Spa will take care of every need. Free tennis lessons. The world's largest pool. Great food. The best of rooms. And those hot, soothing springs. Our low-cost package is perfect for romantic getaways for two: only $2,000 per week.
>
> Call Toll free 1-800-555-5555 today.

> Wilbur Park is a family campground. Swim in the gentle river. Let the kids enjoy the playground. Set up the tent and relax. Picnic tables and hot showers. $20.00 per night. Write Wilbur Park, P.O. Box 1009, Mill Valley, CA 94941. reservenow@wilburpark.com

   Write down the following information for each of these areas.

   **a.** types of activities

   **b.** who the vacation spot suits best

   **c.** cost

   **d.** how to get more information

3. Compare the vacation spots. Which would suit your needs best? Explain.

### More Tips for Travel

1. Write down your travel **agenda.** This is a day-by-day list of activities. It can also include travel information, phone numbers, and times you need to be at places. It is a good way to organize your travel information.

2. Use your phone book skills to find tourist or visitor information offices.

3. Keep a notebook on your trip. Write down the names of restaurants, things you see, and places you enjoy. You can share this information with friends or use it again someday.

4. Use map indexes and map keys to make traveling easier and more fun. Points of interest, such as parks, are on state maps as well as city maps.

This is one person's travel agenda for a weekend in San Diego.

| Date | Activities | Important Information |
|---|---|---|
| Friday, August 3 | Fly to San Diego 10:45 A.M.<br>Spend day with Jim and Patty. | Flight 3432,<br>California Airlines |
| Saturday, August 4 | See Balboa Park.<br>Have dinner with Patrick. | Visitors' Information<br>2688 Mission Bay Drive<br>555-8200<br>Patrick: 555-0988 |
| Sunday, August 5 | Visit Old Town.<br>Have lunch with Arlene and Sue.<br>Go to airport 4:15 P.M. | Arlene: 555-6321<br>Sue: 555-9840<br>Flight 1092 |

Chapter
# 21 Review

## Summary

Use the words and phrases that surround unfamiliar words in a sentence to make an educated guess about their meaning.

Cookbooks are good tools. Use tables of contents and indexes to help you find recipes. Then follow the directions.

There are many resources for planning a trip. Guides, brochures, the Internet, and travel agents are the most important. As always, read for key information and take notes. Compare facts.

| |
|---|
| ingredients |
| agenda |
| brochures |
| entree |
| recipe |
| a la carte |
| reservations |
| toll free |

## Vocabulary Review

**Complete each sentence with a term from the box. Use a separate sheet of paper.**

1. Directions for preparing food in a certain way can be found in a ____.
2. Courses of food that are charged separately are called ____.
3. One way to read about travel is in ____ from a travel agent or auto club.
4. Arrangements to save a place are called ____.
5. A telephone call which costs you nothing is ____.
6. A day-by-day list of activities is called an ____.
7. An ____ is a main course.
8. The ____ are what is found in a prepared food.

## Chapter Quiz

**Answer the following questions in one or two sentences. Use a separate sheet of paper.**

1. What are two ways to find out the meanings of words on a menu?
2. What are two ways to find a recipe for pot roast in a cookbook?
3. A recipe calls for 1 c flour. What does that mean?
4. A recipes calls for 2 lbs tomatoes. What does *lbs* mean?
5. Where are three places you can read about travel?
6. What are two kinds of things to compare when reading about different trips?
7. How can the Internet help you plan a trip?
8. Why is it a good idea to keep a notebook while you are on a trip?

## Critical Thinking

You are taking a trip in your car. How could your English skills help you have a good trip? Give two examples.

### Group Activity

Work with a group to write a plan for a class trip. Where would you like to go? How long will you stay there? What will you do? How does it relate to what you are learning in school? Organize your plan by listing the things you know about the place you are visiting and the things you would like to know. Share your plan with the entire class.

# Unit 7 Review

**Read each sentence below. Then choose the letter that best completes each one.**

**1.** A newspaper headline tells you the
- A. subscription rate.
- B. name of a newspaper.
- C. page where you can find an article.
- D. title of an article.

**2.** The part of a newspaper that tells you where to find an area of the newspaper is the
- A. subscription page.
- B. index.
- C. headline.
- D. current events page.

**3.** All of the following are examples of a hard news story, except a report about
- A. a mud slide in California.
- B. peace talks.
- C. fuel costs.
- D. a dog that can juggle with its nose.

**4.** If you subscribe to a magazine, you
- A. get the magazine delivered to your home.
- B. can buy the magazine for a discount at the store.
- C. buy advertising space in the magazine.
- D. contribute articles to the magazine on a regular basis.

**5.** If you make an educated guess about a word's meaning, you
- A. ask someone who knows.
- B. use your own experience and common sense to figure out what the word might mean.
- C. look the word up in a dictionary.
- D. attend a class to learn the word's meaning.

**6.** All of the following might be included in a list of ingredients, except
- A. $\frac{1}{2}$ c of sugar.
- B. 3 tbl of butter.
- C. mix well for 5 minutes.
- D. 1 egg.

**7.** A good source of travel information is
- A. a brochure.
- B. a guidebook.
- C. the Internet.
- D. all of the above

**Critical Thinking**

What are two or three pros and cons of dining out?

**WRITING** A friend of yours wants to visit the area in which you live. On a separate sheet of paper, write an essay describing a travel agenda for your friend. Include two places your friend could visit and two activities your friend could do with you. Your essay should be at least three paragraphs long.

Unit 8

# English for Personal Expression

Chapter 22
## Writing Personal Messages

Chapter 23
## Using Criticism

*Writing a personal letter or card about a special event like a graduation is an important way of staying in touch with other people. English skills make letter-writing easy.*

Chapter 22

# Writing Personal Messages

## Words to Know

| | |
|---|---|
| **inexpensive** | not too costly |
| **occasion** | a special time or event |
| **sympathy** | a feeling of sadness for someone else |
| **formal** | organized and following rules |
| **RSVP** | a French abbreviation for "please respond" |

### Card Project

A relative has sent you a sweater that you like very much. On a folded sheet of construction paper, design a thank-you card to send to your relative. Be sure to include a personal message, and explain why you like the gift.

### Learning Objectives

- Identify reasons for sending cards.
- Use details to write personal messages in cards and letters.
- Write and answer invitations.

## SKILL 22.1 Add Personal Messages to Cards

Sending cards is an easy thing to do. Cards show that you remember and care about someone. They can cheer up people and make them feel appreciated. Sending cards is an **inexpensive**, or not too costly, way to send a message a long distance. Cards can come in handy for awkward **occasions**, or events. For example, cards expressing **sympathy**, a feeling of sadness, can be sent to the family of a person who died. Cards can also be used to "break the ice" when you want to let someone know you care.

Here are just a few examples of the kinds of cards you can find in stores today.

| | | |
|---|---|---|
| birthday | wedding | anniversary |
| sympathy | graduation | get well |
| Christmas | Hanukkah | Kwanzaa |
| Father's Day | Mother's Day | thank you |

You can, of course, just buy these cards, sign your name, and send them off. Why bother adding personal messages?

There are good reasons for doing this. Personal messages help you show special friendship, caring, and concern. In only a minute or two, you can add extra meaning to your cards.

## Practice

Complete the following activities on a separate sheet of paper.

1. Write two reasons that people do not bother to send cards at all.
2. Write two reasons that people might send cards at special times.
3. Write one reason to add personal messages to cards.

## SKILL 22.2 Make It Personal

There is one key word to writing personal messages—details. Details are often small items or little facts. They do not have to be important.

The details you include in a personal message should have a special meaning for the person to whom you are writing. Here is an example of a personal thank-you message.

> Dear Andy,
>
> The sweater you gave me is lovely. The shade of blue is just perfect. Lots of people have told me I look great in it. Thank you for thinking of me on my birthday.
>
> Sincerely,
> Mary

**Brush Up on the Basics**

You can make your messages more personal by using prepositional phrases as adjectives or adverbs. (See Grammar 52–53 in the Reference Guide.)

Notice the details in Mary's note. Mary mentions the gift (sweater), its color (blue), and how she looks in it (great). When Andy gets the card, he will feel that Mary truly appreciates the sweater.

## Practice

A friend has sent you a CD. On a separate sheet of paper, write the friend a personal thank-you message. Include at least three details to make the message personal.

## SKILL 22.3 Write Personal Messages in Difficult Situations

You are writing a thank-you note for a gift that you really do not like. Perhaps you are sending a sympathy card to a family. What should you say in these difficult situations?

In difficult situations, you need to consider the other person's feelings. Keep the notes short, but show your caring or appreciation. On a sympathy card, you might write something like this: *My thoughts are with you. Let me know if I can help*. You can make it more personal by adding a happy memory. Here is an example.

> *John was a good friend. He was always there when I needed him. I will miss him, too.*

Thank-you notes for unwanted gifts should be kept simple. Just write something like this: *Thanks again for the feathered hat. I'll remember it always.* Don't lie. Remember, it is the thought that counts!

**Everyday English**

If a friend sent you a thank-you note, would you appreciate a personal message? Why or why not?

## Practice

On a separate sheet of paper, write a personal message for one of the following situations.

- Your friend's grandfather has just died.
- Your aunt has given you a book you have wanted to read for a long time.

## SKILL 22.4 How to Write Postcards

You are relaxing on the Hawaiian island of Maui. The beach is long and white. Every day the sun feels better and better. You taste fresh, strange fruits at breakfast. At night, you dance under the stars with a new friend.

The time comes to write a postcard home. You quickly write, *Wish you were here,* and sign your name. After all, what else is there to say?

Actually, there is a lot to say. Details about the trip can make the card more interesting for your family and friends. Read the example of a postcard message on the next page.

Dear Stan,

Hawaii is wonderful. The beaches are long and beautiful. I spend my days tasting tropical fruits and swimming. Tomorrow, I plan to try windsurfing. Oh, by the way, I met someone special. You'll hear more about that when I return. See you on the 16th.

Your friend,
Mike

Before Mike wrote the postcard, he thought about interesting things he had done. He thought about what his friend Stan would find interesting. He picked out a few details and put them on the card. His friend cannot wait to see Mike and ask him about his new friend.

## Practice

In Chapter 21, you wrote a short description of your dream vacation. Now write a postcard home from that vacation. Include at least three made-up details about the trip.

*Sample postcard*

## SKILL 22.5 Write and Answer Invitations

Let's party! This is a phrase many people like to hear. Most of the time, news of a party is passed along by telephone. For a more **formal**, or organized, party, it is a good idea to send out written invitations. That way, you can plan food and drinks for the right number of people.

You can buy printed invitations at most card shops. They usually help you answer the *who, what, why, where, when,* and *how* questions. All you have to do is fill in the blanks. Here is an example.

18th Birthday Party!

For: Alan vos Savant

Where: 1044 Innwood Dr.

When: June 16th

What to wear: Formal

What time? 8:00 p.m.

RSVP by: June 2nd To: (513) 555-3039

Notice the letters **RSVP** at the bottom of the invitation. They stand for *repondez s'il vous plait.* That is French for "please respond." Whenever you receive an invitation, you should always call and let the host know whether you are coming or not. This is considered common courtesy. Otherwise, you may not be invited to any more parties.

**English Tip**
Sometimes, invitations say "Regrets Only" and give a phone number. This means you should call only if you cannot go to the event.

## Practice

Write an invitation to your next birthday party. Make up the details. Be sure to answer the *who, what, why, where, when,* and *how* questions.

## SKILL 22.6 Write Personal Letters

It is easy to pick up the phone and call your family and friends long distance. It is not always easy to pay the phone bill. Sending letters is an inexpensive way to communicate. Letters are also a good place to write about special feelings you have for someone. An e-mail to a friend is one kind of personal letter.

Like personal messages on cards, letters and e-mails should be full of details. If you have been too busy to write, explain why. If you have a new job, explain what you do. You have lots of room in a letter—use it.

Personal letters are less formal than business letters. Just put your own address and date in the upper right corner. Close it with "Sincerely," or "Love," and your name. Remember, if you are taking the trouble to send a card or letter, make it worthwhile. Put a little of yourself into it! Read the personal letter on the next page. Notice the detail and the form.

**English and Technology**

It can be easy just to dash off a quick message and e-mail it to a friend. However, if you take time to edit your e-mail, you can say something really special.

3939 Dakota Street
Worthington, OH 43085
June 4, 2000

Dear Derek,

I'm sorry it's taken me so long to write. I've been really busy. For one thing, I just started a new job. I'm working as a grocery bagger at Green's. I work three hours each afternoon after school. It's a fast pace, so the time passes quickly.

What am I doing with all that money? I'm saving most of it for college. But some of it gets spent on Linda. Yes, I still see Linda. Last week we drove to the mountains and went hiking.

Will you be back in July? Write and let me know the dates. It will be great to see you.

Sincerely,
Stan

**Everyday English**

When is the next chance you will have to write a card or letter? How can you make it personal?

## Practice

Your best friend has moved away. Write him or her a letter on a separate sheet of paper. Explain what has been happening in your life. Include at least ten details. Use the same form as the letter above.

Chapter

# 22 Review

## Summary

| |
|---|
| There are many reasons to send cards. You can make each card more meaningful by writing a personal message inside. |
| Personal messages should be full of details. They may also focus on your feelings. |
| For difficult situations, be honest. Be careful not to hurt anyone's feelings. |
| Invitations should include answers to the *who, what, why, where, when,* and *how* questions. RSVP means that you should let the host know if you are coming or not. |
| Postcards are usually written by people who are traveling. They are more interesting when they include details about the trip and the person's activities. |
| Letters give you a chance to write many details. Personal letters are more informal than business letters. |

| |
|---|
| RSVP |
| occasion |
| formal |
| inexpensive |
| sympathy |

## Vocabulary Review

**Match each term in the box with its meaning. Write the term and its matching number on a separate sheet of paper.**

**1.** not costing too much

**2.** organized and following rules

**3.** a feeling of sorrow for someone else's loss

**4.** a French abbreviation for "please respond"

**5.** a special time or event

## Chapter Quiz

**Answer the following questions in one or two sentences. Use a separate sheet of paper.**

**1.** What are three occasions when you would send a card?

**2.** Why would you write a personal message inside a card?

**3.** What do good personal messages include?

**4.** What is one example of what you would write in a personal thank-you message?

**5.** What is one example of what you would write in a personal message for a sympathy card?

**6.** How can you save money by sending postcards?

**7.** At the bottom of an invitation are the letters *RSVP*. What does this mean, and what should you do?

**8.** What should be included on every invitation?

**9.** What goes in the upper right corner of personal letters?

**10.** What are two ways to close personal letters?

## Critical Thinking

Find an article or book about a place you have never visited. Read a little about it. Take notes. Then write a postcard from that place to your home. Include at least three details about what you are doing or seeing.

## Group Activity

Work with a partner to write and exchange a series of six letters. Each letter should be personal. Include at least two details about your home and school in each letter.

*Giving and receiving criticism is a part of life. Practical English skills help you use criticism to make your life better.*

# Chapter 23 Using Criticism

## Words to Know

| | |
|---|---|
| **criticism** | judgments made about a person or thing |
| **compliments** | positive comments |
| **constructive** | useful |

## Review Project

Think of a movie you have seen recently, and write a review of it. Then read the chapter. After you have finished reading the chapter, look over your review. Use what you have learned to determine if your review was negative or positive.

## Learning Objectives

- Explain the meaning of criticism.
- Describe three uses for criticism in everyday life.
- Use four steps for giving effective criticism.
- Describe the best ways to respond to criticism.

## SKILL 23.1 Recognize Criticism

Perhaps you have seen movies reviewed on TV. The reviewer outlines the good and bad things about a movie. You are hearing **criticism**, or judgments made about this movie.

People often think of criticism as being only bad or negative comments. "You'll never amount to anything," is an example of a negative comment. Criticism may be positive, too. **Compliments**, or positive comments, are a form of criticism. You may look at someone and say, "That haircut is very flattering." You are judging the person's appearance. You are using criticism.

## Practice

Think of one time you received criticism. Was it positive or negative? How did it make you feel? Describe the experience on a separate sheet of paper.

Now think of one time you gave criticism. Was it positive or negative? Did you consider the feelings of the other person? How did that person act? Describe the experience.

**Everyday English**

Do you know someone who uses too much negative criticism?

## SKILL 23.2 Use Criticism in Your Everyday Life

You have personal relationships with many people, such as your family, friends, and co-workers. You also have to live with the things you do and with your own feelings.

Criticism can improve your personal relationships. You can use it to express things you like and dislike about others. If you are clear in your criticism, you can make things change for the better. You can help make sure that the good things continue. You can get your feelings out in the open. How about receiving criticism? You can use self-criticism and criticism from others to improve yourself. Useful criticism is also called **constructive** criticism. People can use it to make their lives better.

### English and Careers

Giving and receiving criticism is an important job skill. Employers value workers who have suggestions for improvement and who want to improve their own work by listening.

### Practice

Use a separate sheet of paper to answer these questions. Write one or two sentences for each one.

1. What is one example of negative criticism?
2. What is one example of positive criticism?
3. Which do you think should be used more often? Why?

## SKILL 23.3 Give Constructive Criticism

Sometimes, giving constructive criticism is easy. You may just want to give someone a compliment. You may know someone well enough that you feel comfortable saying anything to him or her.

Many times, giving constructive criticism can be difficult. For example, Orlando and Shannon are dating. Sometimes Shannon teases Orlando in front of his friends. Orlando is not sure how to ask her to stop. Here are some steps to make it easier.

### Step 1: Think Before You Speak

Do you know someone who complains all the time, no matter what? Do you know someone who says things in anger or just to be mean? That person is not being constructive. The first step in giving constructive criticism is to think before you speak or act. Perhaps this means counting to 10 when you feel angry. Maybe it means running around a track when you feel sad or upset. Getting control of your feelings is really a skill. Only *you* can find what works best for you.

**English Tip**
It often helps to write out your criticisms. This can help you plan what to say and how to say it.

### Step 2: Analyze the Situation

Take the time to analyze the situation. Look for both negative and positive points. In Orlando's case, he does not like it when Shannon teases him. It makes him uncomfortable in front of his friends. There are positive things, too. He likes Shannon. He likes being around her. If he did not, he would not even bother trying to solve the problem.

### Step 3: Decide What You Want

Finally, think about what you would like to see happen. Many times, people complain without a clear purpose. Nothing makes them happy. To give constructive criticism, you should have a goal in mind. In Orlando's case, he wants Shannon to stop teasing him. He hopes they can continue to see each other.

### Step 4: Put It Together

It is time for you to give your criticism. It is a good idea to start off with something positive. Then give the negative criticism. Try not to blame the other person. It is best just to state facts and your feelings. Say what you want to have happen. Try to focus on solving the problem. If the other person gets emotional, stay calm. Here is how Orlando gave Shannon constructive criticism.

**Brush Up on the Basics**

When giving criticism, use subordinating conjunctions to show how your ideas are related to each other. (See Grammar 46 in the Reference Guide.)

**Orlando:** *Shannon, I really like you. In fact, I like our relationship a lot. I want to keep seeing you. That's why I'm bringing this up. Sometimes, I feel uncomfortable when you tease me, especially in front of our friends. What do you think we can do to solve this problem?*

**Shannon:** *So, you don't like me when we're with our friends? You think I am mean?*

**Orlando:** *I like you a lot. I just feel uncomfortable when you tease me. I'd feel better if we could talk about it.*

Notice that Orlando does not blame Shannon. He explains how he feels. He explains what is causing his feelings. He focuses on trying to solve the problem.

## Practice

> **Everyday English**
>
> What is the difference between complaining and giving constructive criticism?

Jill's parents just got divorced. Jill lives with her mother. Jill loves her mother. They have always been more like friends than mother and daughter. Lately, Jill's mother is yelling at her all the time. She says things like, "You dress like a slob. You spend too much time away from home. Why can't you help out more?" One day, Jill feels herself getting ready to lash back at her mother.

On a separate sheet of paper, write what Jill should do or say. Use the four steps for giving constructive criticism.

### Using Criticism

A friend says, "You're my friend. I care about you. I'm telling you this because I think you should know. You have bad breath."

What is the first thing that happens? Maybe you feel embarrassed. Maybe you are hurt. Being able to use criticism is a skill, too, just as giving it is.

When you are criticized, put your feelings aside for a moment. Otherwise, you may not be able to think clearly. Say to yourself, "Is this good information? Can I make myself better in some way by using it?"

What if the criticism is not constructive? You can turn it around. Analyze the situation. Then use some constructive criticism of your own to solve the problem. Sometimes, a person will continue to be critical and complaining, no matter what. In such cases, ignore the criticism. Always take the time to think about it before you do.

### When You Criticize Yourself

Many times, people criticize themselves. Often, it is negative criticism. "I'm no good." "Why did I say that? It was stupid." "I'll never make it." This is negative criticism. It is useless.

Turn your thoughts into constructive criticism. Try using these tips.

1. Pay attention to your thoughts. When you are being negative, stop. Then say something nice about yourself.

2. Give yourself constructive criticism. Do not just think about *what* you need to do better. Think about *how* you can do it better. Solve the problem.

3. When something bad happens, ask yourself, "How can I turn this into something positive?"

4. Be willing to ask for help when you want to change. You will find that most people will admire you for asking.

Chapter

# 23 Review

## Summary

| |
|---|
| Criticism can be positive or negative. Constructive criticism contains a little of both. |
| Constructive criticism can be used to improve your personal relationships. |
| Constructive criticism involves thinking before acting. It means analyzing a situation for good and bad points. There should be a goal to constructive criticism. |
| Try being open to criticism. Think about it, and turn it into something positive. Remember that you can use criticism to make your life better. |

| |
|---|
| constructive |
| compliments |
| criticism |

## Vocabulary Review

**Complete each sentence with a term from the box. Use a separate sheet of paper.**

1. When someone ____ you, these are positive comments.
2. You can use ____ to express things you like and dislike.
3. Criticism becomes ____ when you use it to make your life better.

## Chapter Quiz

**Answer the following questions in one or two sentences. Use a separate sheet of paper.**

1. What is negative criticism? Give an example.
2. What is a compliment? Give an example.
3. What is constructive criticism?
4. How can you use constructive criticism to make your personal life better?
5. You want to think before you act. What are two ways to calm yourself down when you are upset?
6. You are having a problem at work. You decide to analyze the situation. What do you look for?
7. Your friend really bothers you at the movies. He is always shifting in his seat. What would your goal be when giving him constructive criticism?
8. Suppose your friend becomes angry when you give him criticism. What should you do?
9. A friend tells you that you are too noisy at parties. What are two ways to handle this criticism?

## Critical Thinking

Find a review of a restaurant, movie, or play in the newspaper. Separate the comments into "positive" and "negative." Write them on a separate sheet of paper.

### Group Activity

You have a friend who is mean to others. Work with a group to list five ways to give constructive criticism without hurting his or her feelings. Then compare your list with another group's list. Constructively tell the other group how it can improve the list.

# Unit 8 Review

**Read each sentence below. Then choose the letter that best completes each one.**

**1.** One example of a personal message is a

**A.** lease agreement.
**B.** get-well card.
**C.** 1040EZ form.
**D.** schedule.

**2.** If you see the abbreviation *RSVP* on an invitation, you should

**A.** bring a covered dish.
**B.** not bring young children.
**C.** dress in formal clothing.
**D.** tell the person who sent the invitation if you are coming.

**3.** One important tip for writing a personal message on a sympathy card is to make sure you

**A.** keep your note short but show that you care.
**B.** write everything that you know about the person.
**C.** try to change the subject to something more pleasant.
**D.** tell a funny story about something that just happened.

**4.** When you write a party invitation, include

**A.** why you are having a party.
**B.** when the party will be.
**C.** where the party will be.
**D.** all of the above

**5.** Criticism is

**A.** telling someone what you really think of them.
**B.** always negative.
**C.** something to avoid if possible.
**D.** making judgments about a person or thing.

**6.** When making a criticism, you should

**A.** say what you think the person wants to hear.
**B.** say what comes to mind as quickly as you can.
**C.** think before you speak.
**D.** all of the above

**7.** Constructive criticism is criticism that is

**A.** useful.
**B.** mean.
**C.** poorly said.
**D.** always written.

**Critical Thinking**

Why is it important to add a personal message to a card or letter to a friend?

**WRITING** Your sister Claire thinks that her friend Alex is not being a good friend. Alex always interrupts her when she talks. Write an essay in which you give advice to Claire. Tell Claire how she can give constructive criticism to her friend Alex. Your essay should be at least three paragraphs long.

# Appendix

## Glossary

## Reference Guide

## Index

# Glossary

**a la carte** a separate price for each item on a menu

**accomplishments** things done well

**acronym** an abbreviation based on the first letters of words in a title or slogan

**action verbs** words that show action, like *cook* and *run*

**ad copy** spoken or written words in advertising

**agenda** a list of things to do

**almanac** a book published each year that lists many facts, statistics, and other kinds of information

**analyze** to figure something out; to interpret information

**annual fee** a yearly charge

**antidote** a treatment for poisoning

**appendix** additional information found at the back of a book

**application** a form that employers ask job-seekers to fill out with information about themselves

**atlas** a book that contains maps of regions, countries, and continents

**balance** an amount

**ballot** a list of people running for office; also a list of local laws that must be voted on

**benefits** extras, such as health insurance, for workers

**bias** an attitude that is strongly or unfairly on one side of an issue

**birth certificate** an official record that contains a person's family and birth information

**body language** messages given by the body

**brochures** booklets

**call number** the Dewey Decimal number by which a nonfiction book is arranged on a library shelf

**caption** words that tell about an illustration

**car pool** a group of people who share car rides

**card catalog** a computerized or index card file that lists books, magazines, CD-ROMs, and other library sources by title, author, subject, and key word

**check register** a record book for checks

**communication** the giving and receiving of information

**comparative** a word used when saying how two things are alike or different

**compliments** positive comments

**confident** sure of yourself

**cons** reasons against

**constructive** useful

**consumer** a person who buys goods and services

**cover letter** a short letter to an employer included with job application or résumé

**co-workers** people you work with

**credit reference** a person or business that can vouch that you pay your bills

**crisis hotline** an emergency telephone number to call in a serious situation

**criticism** judgments made about a person or thing

**current events** things that are happening now

**deductions** money taken from a paycheck for taxes and other things

**dependent** a person who is supported by another

**deposit** money that is put in an account; to put money in an account

**Dewey Decimal System** a system of numbering library books

**duty** a task performed on a job

**editing** improving writing by making changes

**editorial** a statement of opinion

**election** the choosing of government leaders or local laws by voting

**emotions** feelings

**entree** a main course

**essay test** a test that asks a person to write at least one paragraph on a certain subject

**estimate** a guess at what something will cost

**evidence** proof; statements that back up a claim that something is true

**extension** an additional period of time to file taxes

**external** outside

**fact** information that can be measured or proved as true

**fee** money charged for a service

**fiction** imaginary stories, such as novels and short stories

**formal** organized and following rules

**generic** without a brand name

**glossary** a list of definitions of special words in a section found at the back of a book

**goals** the things a person wants to achieve

**hazard** a danger

**headlines** titles of newspaper or magazine articles

**Health Maintenance Organization** a type of company that provides health care insurance

**human resources department** a company department that hires employees and helps them solve problems

**illustration** a drawing or photograph

**income tax** money you need to pay the government, based on the amount of money you made during the year

**index** a list of subjects and their page numbers found at the back of a book

**inexpensive** not too costly

**ingredients** what a prepared food contains

**interest** the percentage earned or charged on money

**interests** concerns or hobbies

**internal** inside

**intersection** the place where two streets cross each other

**itemize** to list, as tax deductions

**job aid** anything that helps people do their job correctly

**key words** the most important written or spoken words in a sentence, paragraph, or text

**landlord** a person who owns rental property

**lease** a written contract between a landlord and a tenant

**literature** writings that are imaginative

**main idea** the central thought or key piece of information that is written or spoken

**memo** a short note

**minimum** the least amount

**network** the people you contact to help you get information about jobs

**nonfiction** writings about true-to-life events or subjects

**not applicable** does not apply

**objective test** a test that asks a person to choose one answer over another

**obligated** having responsibility for something

**occasion** a special time or event

**opinion** information based on a person's experience or thoughts; not a fact

**organize** to put things into clear order

**periodicals** magazines, newspapers, and journals

**personal reference** a person who can speak in favor of another person's good character

**pharmacist** a person who fills prescriptions

**physician** a medical doctor

**points of interest** interesting things to do and see

**policies** the rules of a company

**prescription** a doctor's order for special medicine

**presentation** the act of showing or explaining something to another person or group

**procedure** the steps you follow to accomplish a task

**product** something for sale that has been manufactured or grown

**pronounce** to say a word out loud

**proofread** to check writing carefully for mistakes

**proposition** a local or state law, or issue, that must be voted on

**pros** reasons for; in favor of

**psychiatrist** a medical doctor who specializes in mental health treatment

**psychologist** a professional who specializes in mental health treatment

**public transportation** vehicles like buses and subways that are available for anyone to use

**recipe** a set of directions for preparing food a certain way

**reference** a person who can say whether a product or service is good or poor

**reference section** a section of a library containing the most-used books of information

**refundable deposit** money that can be returned if certain conditions are met

**register** to sign up

**reservations** arrangements to save a place

**résumé** a written statement of a person's work experience, education, and personal information

**role model** a person you want to be like and learn from

**route** a certain path or direction

**RSVP** a French abbreviation for "please respond"

**scan** to look quickly through written material

**service** a skill that a person offers, such as washing a car

**service contract** a written agreement to provide a service

**short-answer test** a test that asks a person to write one or two sentences to answer a question

**slang** an informal language that is not considered part of correct English

**specialist** a doctor who treats a particular kind of illness

**Statement of Earnings and Deductions** the part of a paycheck stub telling how much money was earned and how much was deducted

**subscribe** to order

**subscription** a form for ordering a magazine or newspaper

**summarize** to explain, in writing or speech, the major events or ideas without using details

**sympathy** a feeling of sadness for someone else

**symptoms** signs of illness

**table of contents** a list of chapters or articles found at the front of a book or magazine

**task** a small part of a large job

**tax deductions** costs that can be subtracted from yearly income to help lower taxable income, such as health care costs

**taxable income** income that is taxed by the government

**tenant** a renter

**toll free** without a charge

**topic sentence** a sentence that introduces the subject or states the purpose

**transaction** an exchange, usually involving money

**trend** a general movement in a certain direction

**utilities** services, such as gas, electricity, and water

**visualization** picturing something

**vouch** to speak in favor of; to say that something is true

**warranty** a guarantee on a product or service

**withheld** held back

# REFERENCE GUIDE

## SENTENCES

GRAMMAR 1

### Definition of a sentence

A sentence is a group of words that expresses a complete thought. Every sentence must have a subject and a predicate. (See Grammar 3–6.) Every sentence begins with a capital letter and ends with a punctuation mark.

The tornado has already killed 40 people.

Is it still raining?

Be careful!

Sometimes a sentence may have only one word. (See Grammar 5.)

Listen. Hurry!

GRAMMAR 2

### Kinds of sentences

There are four different kinds of sentences.

A *declarative sentence* makes a statement. A declarative sentence ends with a period.

A volcano in the Canary Islands is for sale.

An *interrogative sentence* asks a question. An interrogative sentence ends with a question mark.

Who would want to buy a volcano?

An *imperative sentence* gives a command. An imperative sentence ends with a period.

Show me the list of buyers.

An *exclamatory sentence* expresses strong feelings or excitement. An exclamatory sentence ends with an exclamation point.

They must be crazy!

GRAMMAR 3

## Subjects and predicates in declarative sentences

Every sentence has two main parts, the subject and the predicate. The subject names what the sentence is about. The predicate describes an action by or a state of being of the subject.

In most declarative sentences, the subject is the first part. The predicate is the second part.

A famous sea captain (subject) was often sick. (predicate)

He (subject) suffered from seasickness. (predicate)

In some declarative sentences, the predicate is the first part. The subject is the second part.

Back and forth rolled (predicate) the captain's ship. (subject)

GRAMMAR 4

## Subjects and predicates in interrogative sentences

Every interrogative sentence has a subject and a predicate. In some interrogative sentences, the subject is the first part. The predicate is the second part.

Who (subject) solved the mystery? (predicate)

Which clue (subject) was most important? (predicate)

In most interrogative sentences, part of the predicate comes before the subject. To find the subject and predicate, rearrange the words of the interrogative sentence. Use those words to make a declarative sentence. (The declarative sentence will not always sound natural, but it will help you.) The subject and predicate of the two sentences are the same.

Did (predicate) the person (subject) lie about it? (predicate)

(The person (subject) did lie about it?) (predicate)

## GRAMMAR 5 Subjects and predicates in imperative sentences

Only the predicate of an imperative sentence is spoken or written. The subject of the sentence is understood. That subject is always "you."

[You] Try an underhand serve.

[You] Please show me how to do it.

## GRAMMAR 6 Subjects and predicates in exclamatory sentences

Every exclamatory sentence has a subject and a predicate. In most exclamatory sentences, the subject is the first part. The predicate is the second part.

Greenland (subject) is frozen over nearly all of the time! (predicate)

In some exclamatory sentences, part of the predicate comes before the subject.

What terrible weather (predicate) that city (subject) has! (predicate)

(That city (subject) has terrible weather!) (predicate)

## GRAMMAR 7 Compound subjects in sentences

A sentence with a compound subject has two or more subjects with the same predicate.

> Wilbur Wright and his brother Orville developed the first airplane that could fly.
>
> The Spirit of St. Louis, the Enola Gay, and Air Force One are all famous airplanes.

## GRAMMAR 8 Compound predicates in sentences

A sentence with a compound predicate has two or more predicates with the same subject.

> The postal workers took in the tailless cat and named him Kojak.
>
> Kojak lives in the post office, catches mice, and plays with yarn.

## GRAMMAR 9 Compound sentences

A compound sentence is made up of two shorter sentences joined by a coordinating conjunction. (See Grammar 45.) A compound sentence has a subject and a predicate followed by another subject and another predicate.

> G. David Howard set a record in 1978, and it remains unbroken.
>
> Howard told jokes for more than 13 hours, but few of them were funny.

## NOUNS

GRAMMAR 10

### Definition of a noun

A noun is a word that names a person, place, thing, event, or idea.

That brave man crossed the ocean in a rowboat.

GRAMMAR 11

### Singular and plural forms of nouns

Almost every noun has two forms. The singular form names one person, place, thing, event, or idea.

Only one worker in that factory can name the secret ingredient.

The plural form names more than one person, place, thing, event, or idea.

Several workers in those two factories can name the secret ingredients.

GRAMMAR 12

### Spelling plural forms of nouns

For most nouns, add *-s* to the singular form to make the plural form.

joke—jokes

character—characters

cartoon—cartoons

If the singular form ends in *s, ss, sh, ch, z,* or *x*, add *-es*.

bus—buses

witch—witches

kiss—kisses

fox—foxes

wish—wishes

buzz—buzzes

If the singular form ends in a consonant and *y*, change the *y* to *i* and add *-es*.

spy—spies　　discovery—discoveries

mystery—mysteries

If the singular form ends in *f*, usually change the *f* to *v* and add *-es*. If the singular form ends in *fe*, usually change the *f* to *v* and add *-s*. There are some important exceptions to these rules. Look in a dictionary if you are not sure of the correct plural form.

half—halves　　wife—wives

loaf—loaves　　knife—knives

Some exceptions

roof—roofs　　chief—chiefs　　safe—safes

If the singular form ends in *o*, add *-s* to some words and *-es* to others. Look in a dictionary if you are not sure of the correct plural form.

studio—studios　　tomato—tomatoes

piano—pianos　　potato—potatoes

zero—zeros　　hero—heroes

Some nouns change in other ways to make the plural form.

child—children　　mouse—mice

woman—women　　goose—geese

A few nouns have the same singular form and plural form.

sheep—sheep　　deer—deer

moose—moose　　series—series

GRAMMAR 13

## Common nouns and proper nouns

A common noun is a word that names any person, place, thing, event, or idea.

> Then the man stopped in a small town and ate a hamburger.

A proper noun is a word that names a particular person, place, thing, event, or idea. Each word in a proper noun begins with a capital letter.

> Then Max stopped in Junctionville and ate a Big Burger Special on Memorial Day.

GRAMMAR 14

## Possessive nouns

The possessive form of a noun shows ownership. Usually the possessive form of a noun is made by adding an apostrophe and *-s*. (See Punctuation 20.)

> A piranha's teeth are as sharp as razors.

The possessive form of a plural noun that ends in *s* is made by adding only an apostrophe. (See Punctuation 20.)

> Nobody believed the explorers' story.

GRAMMAR 15

## Nouns of address

A noun of address names the person being spoken to. One or two commas separate a noun of address from the rest of a sentence. (See Punctuation 9.)

> Where are you going, Andy?
>
> I told you, Susie, that I have a rehearsal tonight.

## GRAMMAR 16 Appositive nouns

An appositive noun renames or identifies the noun that comes before it in a sentence. An appositive noun is usually part of a group of words. The whole group of words is called an appositive. One or two commas separate an appositive from the rest of a sentence. (See Punctuation 10.)

A convertible was the preferred car of John Jones, the famous *boxer*.

His sister, the *president* of her own company, wanted to ride with him.

# VERBS

## GRAMMAR 17 Definition of a verb

A verb is a word that expresses action or being.

The volcano erupted suddenly.

It was a terrific surprise.

Almost all verbs have different forms, called tenses, to show differences in time (past, present, and future).

Last week puffs of smoke rose from the volcano.

Sometimes a huge cloud of heavy gray smoke rises from the volcano.

Lava probably will rise from the volcano tomorrow.

## GRAMMAR 18 Action verbs

Most verbs are action verbs. An action verb expresses physical action or mental action.

The committee members banned Funky Cat comic books.

They disliked comic books.

## GRAMMAR 19 Linking verbs

Some verbs are linking verbs. A linking verb tells what the sentence subject is or is like. The most common linking verb is the verb *to be.* (See Grammar 23.)

That black and white dog is a mail carrier in California.

The dog's name was Dorsey.

## GRAMMAR 20 Verb phrases

A verb phrase is made up of one or more helping verbs and a main verb that function together in a sentence. The final verb in a verb phrase is the main verb.

The 13,000-pound bell has *disappeared.*

Somebody must have *stolen* it.

The verbs before the main verb in a verb phrase are helping verbs. The most common helping verbs are forms of *be (is, are, am, was, were),* forms of *have (has, have, had),* and forms of *do (does, do, did).* (See Grammar 23.)

That radio station *is* sponsoring a contest.

The station *has* already received 45,217 postcards.

GRAMMAR 21

## Agreement of verbs with nouns

Verb forms that show action or being at the present time are in the present tense. The present tense can also show repeated action. Almost all present tense verbs have two different forms. These two different forms go with different sentence subjects. The verb in a sentence, or the first helping verb in a sentence, must agree with the most important word in the subject of that sentence.

One present tense form of a verb agrees with singular nouns. This verb form ends with *s*.

> A tick **sucks** blood from larger animals.

The other present tense form of a verb agrees with plural nouns.

> Ticks **suck** blood from larger animals.

GRAMMAR 22

## Agreement of verbs with compound subjects

The present tense verb form that agrees with plural nouns also agrees with compound subjects. (See Grammar 7.)

> Beth Obermeyer and her daughter Kristen **hold** a record for long-distance tap dancing.

GRAMMAR 23

## Forms of the verb *be*

The verb *to be* has more forms than other verbs. It has three present tense forms: *is, are,* and *am. Is* agrees with singular nouns. *Are* agrees with plural nouns. *Am* agrees with the pronoun *I.*

Beth Ash is a famous gymnast.

Many people are her fans.

I am a pretty good gymnast, too.

Most verbs have one past tense form that tells about action or existence in the past. The verb *to be* has two past tense forms: *was* and *were. Was* agrees with singular noun subjects. *Were* agrees with plural noun subjects.

The argument was noisy.

Several neighbors were very angry about it.

GRAMMAR 24

## Irregular verbs

Usually the past tense form of a verb ends in *-d* or *-ed.*

William Baxter invented an important part of the Morse code.

John danced the polka.

Some verbs change in other ways to form the past tense. These are called irregular verbs. Look in a dictionary if you are not sure of the correct past tense form of a verb.

Samuel Morse took all the credit.
(past tense of take)

## PRONOUNS

GRAMMAR 25

### Personal pronouns

A personal pronoun identifies the speaker, the person spoken to, or the person or thing spoken about.

> Regis Casement tried to enlist in the Army during World War II, but he was found unfit to serve.

GRAMMAR 26

### Subject forms and object forms of personal pronouns

Most personal pronouns have a subject form and an object form. These different forms are used in different ways in sentences. These are the subject forms of personal pronouns: *I, you, he, she, it, we, they.* These are the object forms of personal pronouns: *me, you, him, her, it, us, them.* (The pronouns *it* and *you* are the same in the subject form and the object form.)

> He could not read the eye chart.

> The army did not accept him.

GRAMMAR 27

### Antecedents of pronouns

A personal pronoun refers to the noun it replaces. That noun is the antecedent of the pronoun.

> Kevin Killen became famous in movies. He was usually accompanied by his guitar, Chance.
> (*Kevin Killen* is the antecedent.)

If a personal pronoun takes the place of two or more nouns, those nouns together are the antecedent of the pronoun.

> Kevin Killen and Oscar Roth often worked together. They made dozens of movies.
>
> (*Kevin Killen and Oscar Roth* is the antecedent.)

---

GRAMMAR 28

## Subject-verb agreement with personal pronouns.

The present tense verb form that agrees with singular nouns also agrees with the pronoun subjects, *he, she,* and *it.*

> She tests new planes.

The present tense verb form that agrees with plural nouns also agrees with the pronoun subjects *I, you, we,* and *they.*

> They test new planes.

---

GRAMMAR 29

## Indefinite pronouns

A word that refers to a general group but does not have a specific antecedent is an indefinite pronoun.

> Nobody can be right about everything.

One common indefinite pronoun, *no one,* is written as two words.

## GRAMMAR 30 Subject-verb agreement with indefinite pronouns

The present tense verb form that agrees with singular nouns also agrees with most indefinite pronouns.

Almost everyone remembers the Alamo.

No one knows exactly what happened there.

**Exception:** Several of the histories tell different stories.

## GRAMMAR 31 Possessive pronouns

A pronoun that shows ownership is a possessive pronoun.

These possessive pronouns are used before nouns in sentences: *my, your, his, her, its, our, their.*

Why are my gym shoes in your locker?

These possessive pronouns stand alone in sentences: *mine, ours, his, hers, its, ours, theirs.*

Are these gym shoes mine, or are they yours?

Unlike possessive nouns, possessive pronouns are not written with apostrophes.

## GRAMMAR 32 Reflexive pronouns

A pronoun that refers back to a noun or pronoun in the same sentence is called a reflexive pronoun. These words are reflexive pronouns: *myself, yourself, himself, herself, itself, ourselves, yourselves, themselves.*

The witness had been talking to himself.

You should have bought yourself a ticket.

## GRAMMAR 33 Demonstrative pronouns

A word that points out one or more people or things is called a demonstrative pronoun. These words can be demonstrative pronouns: *this, that, these,* and *those.*

These are the funniest cartoons.

Nobody laughed at those.

If the word *this, that, these,* or *those* is followed by a noun, the word is not a demonstrative pronoun.

This book includes some funny cartoons.

# ADJECTIVES

## GRAMMAR 34 Definition of an adjective

A word that describes a noun or pronoun is called an adjective. Adjectives usually tell what kind, which one, or how many.

Those two exhausted men have been playing tennis for nine hours.

Adjectives that tell what kind can sometimes stand alone.

They were exhausted.

Adjectives that tell which or how many always come before nouns.

Both players used several rackets.

GRAMMAR 35

## The adjectives *a* and *an*

The adjectives *a* and *an* are usually called *indefinite articles.* (The adjective *the* is usually called a *definite article.*) The adjective *a* is used before words that begin with consonants or with the sound "yew."

A penguin cannot fly

Cooking is a useful activity.

The adjective *an* is used before words that begin with vowels or with a silent *h.*

An ostrich cannot fly.

Denzel is an honorable man.

GRAMMAR 36

## Predicate adjectives

An adjective that comes after a linking verb and adds to the meaning of the subject of the sentence is a predicate adjective.

Maria Spelterina must have been brave.

Her tightrope walks across the Niagara Falls were dangerous.

## GRAMMAR 37 Proper adjectives

An adjective that is formed from a proper noun is a proper adjective. Each word in a proper adjective begins with a capital letter.

The American dollar is worth less than the British pound.

The new Martin Lynch film is great!

## GRAMMAR 38 Comparative and superlative forms of adjectives.

Adjectives can be used to compare two or more people, places, things, events, or ideas. When only two nouns are compared, use the comparative form of an adjective. To make the comparative form, add *-er* to an adjective with one and sometimes two syllables. Use *more* (or *less*) before most adjectives with two or more syllables. Look in a dictionary if you are not sure of the correct comparative form of an adjective.

George is older than Liza.

Hanif is funnier than Virginia.

Lyle is more amusing than Shawn.

Mike was less successful than Patty.

When three or more people, places, things, events, or ideas are compared, use the superlative form of an adjective. To make the superlative form, add *-est* to an adjective with one syllable and many adjectives with two syllables. Use *most* (or *least*) before some adjectives with two syllables and all adjectives with more than two syllables. Look in a dictionary if you are not sure of the correct superlative form of an adjective.

That is the oldest tree I ever saw.

Hanif is the funniest friend I've ever had.

Hanif is the most amusing friend I've ever had.

That is the least interesting story I ever heard.

The comparative and superlative forms of the adjective *good* are *better* and *best.*

Hanif is a better joke-teller than I am.

Hanif is the best joke-teller I have ever known.

The comparative and superlative forms of the adjective *bad* are *worse* and *worst.*

*The Morning Walk* was a worse movie than *The Files.*

*The Morning Walk* was probably the worst movie ever made.

## ADVERBS

GRAMMAR 39

### Definition of an adverb

A word that tells more about a verb or verb phrase is an adverb. Adverbs usually tell *when, where, how,* or *how often.*

The rodeo rider bravely mounted the mustang again.

## GRAMMAR 40 Comparative and superlative forms of adverbs

Adverbs can be used to compare two or more actions. When only two actions are compared, use the comparative form of an adverb. To make the comparative form, usually use *more* (or *less*) before the adverb. Add *-er* to a few short adverbs.

> Polly speaks more clearly than that other parrot.
>
> Polly can fly higher than that other parrot.

When more than two actions are compared, use the superlative form, usually use *most* (or *least*) before the adverb. Add *-est* to a few short adverbs.

> Of all those parrots, Polly speaks most clearly.
>
> Of all those parrots, Polly can fly highest.

The comparative and superlative forms of the adverb *well* are *better* and *best*.

> That parrot behaved better than your pet cat.
>
> Of all the unusual pets in the show, the parrot behaved the best.

The comparative and superlative forms of the adverb *badly* are *worse* and *worst*.

> Your pet monkey behaved worse than that parrot.
>
> Of all the unusual pets in the show, your cat behaved the worst.

## GRAMMAR 41 Using adjectives and adverbs

Use an adjective to add to the meaning of a noun or a pronoun.

> The proud actor accepted the prize.

Use an adverb to add to the meaning of a verb or a verb phrase. Many (but not all) adverbs end in *-ly*.

> The actor accepted the prize proudly.

## GRAMMAR 42 The adverb *not*

The adverb *not* changes the meaning of the verb or verb phrase in a sentence.

> The soldiers in the fort would not surrender.
>
> Help did not arrive in time.

## GRAMMAR 43 Avoiding double negatives

The adverb *not* is a negative word. Other common negative words are *no, never, no one, nobody, nothing, nowhere, hardly, barely,* and *scarcely.* Use only one negative word to make a sentence mean *no* or *not.*

> No one understands how I feel.
>
> My friends never understand how I feel.
>
> Hardly anyone understands how I feel.

## GRAMMAR 44 Adverbs used as intensifiers

Some adverbs add extra emphasis to the meaning of adjectives or other adverbs. These special adverbs are sometimes called intensifiers.

> One terribly nosy neighbor heard the whole conversation.
>
> Very nervously, she told the police all about it.

# CONJUNCTIONS

## GRAMMAR 45 Coordinating conjunctions

A word that is used to join words, phrases, or sentences is a coordinating conjunction. The most common coordinating conjunctions are *but, and,* and *or.*

> Many people have driven across the country, but these two men did it the hard way.
>
> Charles Creighton and James Hargis drove across the country and back again.
>
> They never stopped the engine or took the car out of reverse gear.

GRAMMAR 46

## Subordinating conjunctions and complex sentences

One or more words used to begin a dependent clause is a subordinating conjunction. Some of the most common subordinating conjunctions are listed below.

| | | | |
|---|---|---|---|
| after | before | though | when |
| although | if | unless | whenever |
| because | since | until | while |

A dependent clause is a group of words that has a subject and a predicate but cannot stand alone as a sentence. It functions like an adverb. It tells *when, where, how,* or *why.* A dependent clause usually comes at the end or at the beginning of a sentence. (See Punctuation 8.) A sentence formed from a dependent clause (which cannot stand alone) and a main clause (which can stand alone) is called a *complex sentence.*

Otto E. Funk played his violin while he walked from New York City to San Francisco.

When he finished his musical journey, both his feet and his hands were tired.

Whenever it is threatened, an opossum plays dead.

If you poke it, pick it up, and even roll it over, it remains completely still.

## INTERJECTIONS

GRAMMAR 47 **Definition of an interjection**

A word that simply expresses emotion is an interjection. A comma or an exclamation point separates an interjection from the rest of a sentence. (See Punctuation 11.)

Oh, now it makes sense.

Wow! That is terrific news!

## PREPOSITIONS

GRAMMAR 48 **Definition of a preposition**

A word that shows the relationship of a noun or pronoun to some other word in a sentence is a preposition. Some of the most common prepositions are listed below.

| | | | |
|---|---|---|---|
| about | before | during | over |
| above | behind | for | since |
| across | below | from | through |
| after | beneath | in | to |
| against | beside | into | under |
| along | between | like | until |
| among | beyond | of | up |
| around | by | off | upon |
| at | down | on | with |

## GRAMMAR 49 Prepositional phrases

A preposition is followed by a noun or a pronoun. The preposition and the noun or pronoun that follows it form a prepositional phrase.

A new record for the high jump was set by Dr. David G. Jones.

His family and friends were very proud of him.

Often, other words come between the preposition and the noun or pronoun. Those words are also part of the prepositional phrase.

He set a new record for one-handed pull-ups.

## GRAMMAR 50 Objects of prepositions

The noun or pronoun at the end of a prepositional phrase is the object of that preposition.

One of the main characters of *Chicago Harbor* did not appear until the second season.

## GRAMMAR 51 Personal pronouns in prepositional phrases

A personal pronoun that is the object of a preposition should be in the object form. These are object form pronouns: *me, you, him, her, it, us them.*

The other presents for her are still on the table.

The most interesting present is from me.

GRAMMAR 52

## Prepositional phrases used as adjectives

Some prepositional phrases are used as adjectives. They add to the meaning of a noun or pronoun in a sentence.

> The Caribbean island of Martinique is a department of the French government.

GRAMMAR 53

## Prepositional phrases used as adverbs

Some prepositional phrases are used as adverbs. They add to the meaning of the verb or verb phrase in a sentence, answering the questions *when, where, how,* or *how often.*

> In 1763, Napoleon Bonaparte's wife, Josephine, was born on Martinique.

# SENTENCE PARTS

GRAMMAR 54

## Simple subjects

The most important noun or pronoun in the subject of a sentence is called the simple subject of that sentence.

> A 27-year-old man from Oklahoma swam the entire length of the Mississippi River.
>
> He spent a total of 742 hours in the river.

## GRAMMAR 55 Simple predicates

The verb or verb phrase of a sentence is the simple predicate of that sentence.

> Actor Keyshawn Adams may have had 700 separate savings accounts.
>
> Adams used a different name for each account.

## GRAMMAR 56 Direct objects

A noun or pronoun that receives the action of a verb is the direct object of that verb. A personal pronoun that is a direct object should be in the object form. These are object form pronouns: *me, you, him, her, it, us, them.*

> The cat chased mice.
>
> It did not catch them.

## GRAMMAR 57 Indirect objects

A noun or pronoun that tells *to whom* (or *what*) or *for whom* (or *what*) something is done is the indirect object of the verb. An indirect object comes before a direct object and is not part of a prepositional phrase. A personal pronoun that is a direct object should be in the object form. These are object form pronouns: *me, you, him, her, it, us, them.*

> Professor Sommers gave his students the same lecture every year.
>
> He told them a familiar story.

GRAMMAR 58

## Predicate nominatives

A noun or pronoun that follows a linking verb and renames the sentence subject is the predicate nominative of a sentence. A personal pronoun that is a predicate nominative should be in the subject form. These are subject form pronouns: *I, you, he, she, it, we, they.*

The best candidate was Andrea.

It was she who deserved to win.

## CAPITALIZATION RULES

CAPITALIZATION 1

### First word in a sentence

Begin the first word in every sentence with a capital letter.

Who won the eating contest?

That man ate 17 bananas in two minutes.

CAPITALIZATION 2

### Personal pronoun *I*

Write the pronoun *I* with a capital letter.

At the last possible minute, I changed my mind.

CAPITALIZATION 3

## Names and initials of people

Almost always, begin each part of a person's name with a capital letter.

Tina Menendez    Emily Delancy

Latifah Johnson

Some names have more than one capital letter. Other names have parts that are not capitalized. Check the correct way to write each person's name. (Look in a reference book, or ask the person.)

Rayford O'Hara    Tony de la Cruz

Jeannie D'Antonio

Use a capital letter to write an initial that is part of a person's name.

B. J. Gallardo    J. Kelly Hunt

John F. Kennedy

CAPITALIZATION 4

## Titles of people

Begin the title before a person's name with a capital letter.

Mr. Sam Yee    Captain Cook

Dr. Watson    Governor Anna Long

Do not use a capital letter if the title is used as a common noun.

Did you call the doctor?

Who will be our state's next governor?

CAPITALIZATION 5

## Names of relatives

A word like *grandma* or *uncle* may be used in place of a person's name or as part of a person's name. Begin this kind of word with a capital letter.

> Only Dad and Aunt Ellie understand it.

Usually, if a possessive pronoun comes before a word like *grandma* or *uncle,* do not begin that word with a capital letter.

> Only my dad and my aunt understand it.

CAPITALIZATION 6

## Names of days

Begin the name of each day of the week with a capital letter.

> Many people do not have to work on Saturday or Sunday.

CAPITALIZATION 7

## Names of months

Begin the name of each month of the year with a capital letter.

> At the equator, the hottest months are March and September.

CAPITALIZATION 8

## Names of holidays

Begin each important word in the name of a holiday with a capital letter. Small words like *the* and *of* do not begin with capital letters.

> They usually have a picnic on the Fourth of July and a fancy dinner party on Thanksgiving.

CAPITALIZATION 9

## Names of streets and highways

Begin each word in the name of a street or highway with a capital letter.

> Why is Lombard Street known as the most crooked road in the world?

CAPITALIZATION 10

## Names of cities and towns

Begin each word in the name of a city or town with a capital letter.

> In 1967, the Panthers moved from Brooklyn to Chattanooga.

CAPITALIZATION 11

## Names of states, countries, and continents

Begin each word in the name of a state, country, or continent with a capital letter.

> The story was set in Nevada, but they shot the film in Mexico.
>
> There are very high mountain peaks in Antarctica.

CAPITALIZATION 12

## Names of mountains and bodies of water

Begin each word in the name of a mountain, river, lake, or ocean with a capital letter.

> Amelia Earhart's plane was lost somewhere over the Pacific Ocean.

CAPITALIZATION 13

## Abbreviations

If the spelled-out word begins with a capital letter, begin the abbreviation with a capital letter too.

> On the scrap of paper, the victim had written, "On Wed. see Dr. Lau."

CAPITALIZATION 14

## Titles of works

Use a capital letter to begin the first word, the last word, and every main word in the title of a work. The words *the, a,* and *an* do not begin with capital letters except at the beginning of a title.

Coordinating conjunctions and prepositions also do not begin with capital letters. (See Grammar 45 and Grammar 48.)

> Mike and Alisia were the main characters in the television series *Faulkerson's Place.*

CAPITALIZATION 15

## Other proper nouns

Begin each important word in a proper noun with a capital letter. A proper noun is a word that names a particular person, place, thing, event, or idea. (See Grammar 13.) Usually, the words *the, a,* and *an,* coordinating conjunctions, and prepositions do not begin with capital letters. (See Grammar 45 and Grammar 48.)

> Keenan rushed to the Burger Barn and ordered three Jumbos.

## CAPITALIZATION 16 Proper adjectives

Begin each word in a proper adjective with a capital letter. A proper adjective is an adjective that is formed from a proper noun. (See Grammar 37.)

> That American author writes about English detectives.
>
> She loves Francis Malle movies.

## CAPITALIZATION 17 Direct quotations

Begin the first word of a direct quotation with a capital letter. (See Punctuation 14–16.)

> Dr. Pavlik said, "Her ankle is sprained, but not broken."

If the words that identify who is speaking come in the middle of a quoted sentence, do not begin the second part of a quotation with a capital letter.

> "Her ankle is sprained," said Dr. Pavlik, "but not broken."

## CAPITALIZATION 18 Greetings and closings in letters

Begin the first word in the greeting of a letter with a capital letter.

> Dear Mr. Lincoln: Dear Uncle Abe,

Begin the first word in the closing of a letter with a capital letter.

> Sincerely yours, Very truly yours,
>
> Love,

CAPITALIZATION 19

## Outlines

Begin the first word of each heading of an outline with a capital letter.

II. Garages by mail order

  A. First sold by Dunbar, Inc., in 1922

    1. Build-it-yourself kits

    2. Included all materials and instructions

  B. Other companies now in business

In an outline, use capital Roman numerals to label main ideas. Use capital letters to label supporting ideas. For ideas under supporting ideas, use Arabic numerals. For details, use small letters. Use a period after each Roman numeral, capital letter, Arabic numeral, and small letter.

I. Miner George Warren's wager

  A. Risked his share of Copper Queen mine in bet

    1. Bet on race against George Atkins

      a. Warren on foot

      b. Atkins on horseback

    2. Lost property worth $20 million

## PUNCTUATION RULES

PUNCTUATION 1

### Periods, question marks, and exclamation points at the ends of sentences

Use a period, a question mark, or an exclamation point at the end of every sentence. Do not use more than one of these marks at the end of a sentence. For example, do not use both a question mark and an exclamation point, or do not use two exclamation points.

Use a period at the end of a declarative sentence (a sentence that makes a statement).

> A hockey player must be able to skate backward at top speed.

Use a period at the end of an imperative sentence (a sentence that gives a command).

> Keep your eye on the puck.

Use a question mark at the end of an interrogative sentence (a sentence that asks a question).

> Who is the goalie for their team?

Use an exclamation point at the end of an exclamatory sentence (a sentence that expresses strong feelings or excitement).

> That was a terrific block!

PUNCTUATION 2

## Periods with abbreviations

Use a period at the end of each part of an abbreviation.

Most titles used before people's names are abbreviations. These abbreviations may be used in formal writing. (*Miss* is not an abbreviation and does not end with a period.)

Dr. Desmond Blackwell   Mr. Bob Tilden

Ms. Joan Connolly   Gov. Abraham Tilsett

Most other abbreviations may be used in addresses, notes, and informal writing. They should not be used in formal writing.

Lake View Blvd.   Mon. and Thurs.

Fifth Ave.   Dec. 24

Do not use periods in the abbreviations of names of government agencies, labor unions, and certain other organizations.

Tomorrow night Channel 32 will broadcast a special program about the FBI.

Do not use periods after two-letter state abbreviations in addresses. This kind of abbreviation has two capital letters and no period. Use these abbreviations in addresses.

Their new address is 1887 West Third Street, Los Angeles, CA 90048.

PUNCTUATION 3

## Periods after initials

Use a period after an initial that is part of a person's name.

Chester A. Arthur    C.C. Pyle

Susan B. Anthony

PUNCTUATION 4

## Commas in dates

Use a comma between the number of the day and the number of the year in a date.

Mo Green hit his first home run on April 27, 1998.

If the date does not come at the end of a sentence, use another comma after the number of the year.

April 27, 1998, was an exciting day for his fans.

Do not use a comma in a date that has only the name of a month and the number of a year.

Green hit his final home run in July 2000.

Do not use a comma in a date that has only the name of a month and the number of a day.

April 27 is the anniversary of Green's first home run.

PUNCTUATION 5

## Commas in place names

Use a comma between the name of a city or town and the name of a state or country.

America's tallest building stands in Chicago, Illinois.

If the two names do not come at the end of a sentence, use another comma after the name of the state or country.

Chicago, Illinois, is the home of America's tallest building.

PUNCTUATION 6

## Commas in compound sentences

Use a comma before the conjunctions *and, but,* or *or* in a compound sentence. (See Grammar 9 and Grammar 45.)

Eighteen people tried, but no one succeeded.

PUNCTUATION 7

## Commas in series

Three or more words or groups of words used the same way in a sentence form a series. Use commas to separate the words or word groups in a series.

Jamie, Mitch, Kim, Lou, and Pablo entered the contest.

Each contestant swam one mile, bicycled two miles, and ran five miles.

## Commas after introductory phrases and clauses

PUNCTUATION 8

Use a comma after a phrase that comes before the subject of a sentence. A phrase is a group of words that usually functions as an adjective or an adverb. One kind of phrase is a prepositional phrase. (See Grammar 49.)

In the old dresser, Penny found the diamonds.

If the entire predicate comes before the subject of the sentence, do not use a comma. (See Grammar 3.)

In the old dresser lay the diamonds.

Use a comma after an adverb clause at the beginning of a sentence. (See Grammar 46.)

When he was first named the league's most valuable player, Pavel London was only 18 years old.

## Commas with nouns of address

PUNCTUATION 9

Use a comma after a noun of address at the beginning of a sentence. (See Grammar 15.)

Fernando, that was a terrific pitch!

Use a comma before a noun of address at the end of a sentence.

That was a terrific pitch, Fernando!

If the noun of address comes in the middle of a sentence, use one comma before the noun and another comma after it.

That, Fernando, was a terrific pitch!

PUNCTUATION 10

## Commas with appositives

Use a comma before an appositive at the end of a sentence. (See Grammar 16.)

This costume was worn by Maria Lopez, Hollywood's first Detective Pierce.

If an appositive comes in the middle of a sentence, use one comma before the appositive and another comma after it.

Maria Lopez, Hollywood's first Detective Pierce, wore this costume.

PUNCTUATION 11

## Commas or exclamation points with interjections

Usually use a comma after an interjection. (See Grammar 47.)

Well, we should probably think about it.

Use an exclamation point after an interjection that expresses excitement.

Wow! That's a terrific idea!

PUNCTUATION 12

## Commas after greetings in friendly letters

Use a comma after the greeting in a friendly letter.

Dear John,     Dear Uncle Theodore,

PUNCTUATION 13

## Commas after closings in friendly letters and business letters

Use a comma after the closing in a letter.

Love,    Yours sincerely,

PUNCTUATION 14

## Quotation marks with direct quotations

A direct quotation tells the exact words a person said. Use quotation marks at the beginning and at the end of each part of a direct quotation.

"Look!" cried Moesha. "That cat is smiling!"

"Of course," said Brandon. "It's a Cheshire cat."

PUNCTUATION 15

## Commas with direct quotations

A comma is usually used to separate the words of a direct quotation from the words that tell who is speaking. (See Punctuation 16.)

Jay asked, "Who won the game last night?"

"The Skyhawks won it," said Linda, "in 14 innings."

PUNCTUATION 16

## End punctuation with direct quotations

At the end of a direct quotation, use a period, a comma, a question mark, or an exclamation point before the closing quotation marks.

If the direct quotation makes a statement or gives a command at the end of a sentence, use a period.

Linda said, "The Skyhawks won last night's game."

Jay said, "Tell us about the game."

If the direct quotation makes a statement or gives a command before the end of a sentence, use a comma.

"The Skyhawks won last night's game," said Linda.

"Tell us about the game," Jay said.

If the direct quotation asks a question, use a question mark.

"Was it an exciting game?" asked Jay.

If the direct quotation expresses excitement, use an exclamation point.

Linda exclaimed, "It was great!"

PUNCTUATION 17

## Quotation marks with titles of works

Use quotation marks around the title of a story, poem, song, essay, or chapter.

> "Happy Birthday to You" is the best-known song in the world.

If a period or a comma comes after the title, put the period or comma inside the closing quotation mark.

> The best-known song in the world is "Happy Birthday to You."

PUNCTUATION 18

## Underlines with titles of works

Underline the title of a book, play, magazine, movie, television series, or newspaper. If you are writing on a computer, these titles should be set in italics.

> One of the best movies about baseball was <u>The Last Out.</u>

PUNCTUATION 19

## Apostrophes in contractions

Use an apostrophe in place of the missing letter or letters in a contraction.

> Is not—isn't  I will—I'll

PUNCTUATION 20

## Apostrophes in possessive nouns

Use an apostrophe and *-s* to write the possessive form of a singular noun. (See Grammar 14.)

> This cage belongs to one bird. It is the bird's cage.
>
> This cage belongs to Tweeter. It is Tweeter's cage.

Use only an apostrophe to write the possessive form of a plural noun that ends in *-s*.

This is a club for boys. It is a boys' club.

Use an apostrophe and *-s* to write the possessive form of a plural noun that does not end in *-s*.

This is a club for men. It is a men's club.

PUNCTUATION 21

## Colons after greetings in business letters.

Use a colon after the greeting in a business letter.

Dear Mrs. Huan: Dear Madam or Sir:

Dear Senator Johnson:

PUNCTUATION 22

## Colons in expressions of time

When you use numerals to write time, use a colon between the hour and the minutes.

5:45 P.M. 9:00 A.M. 12:17 P.M.

PUNCTUATION 23

## Hyphens in numbers and fractions

Use a hyphen in a compound number from twenty-one to ninety-nine.

thirty-seven fifty-eight seventy-three

Use a hyphen in a fraction.

one-quarter two-thirds seven-eighths

# Index

# Photo Credits

Cary Wolinsky, Stock Boston, 2; Superstock, 16; Jeff Greenberg, Unicorn, 27; Kenneth Gabrielsen, Liaison International, 30; Jose Pelaez, The Stock Market, 46; Robert Brenner, PhotoEdit, 58; Index Stock Imagery, 68; Jim Whitmer Photography, 82; Patrick Ray Dunn, 96; Bob Daemmrich, Stock Boston, 108; David Young-Wolf, PhotoEdit, 118; Michael Newman, PhotoEdit, 130; Melanie Carr, Uniphoto, 138; Stephanie Rausser, FPG International, 150; Michael Paras, International Stock, 162; Bob Daemmrich, Stock Boston/PictureQuest, 176; Bob Daemmrich, Stock Boston, 192; Uniphoto, 204; Bob Daemmrich, Stone, 220; Stephen Saks, Photo Researchers, 232; Gary Conner, PhotoEdit, 244; Doug Sokell, Visuals Unlimited, 256; Jeff Greenberg, Visuals Unlimited, 270; Ellen Senisi, The Image Works, 282; cover: keyboard: Novastock, Photo Researchers; job application and newspaper: Pearson Education Photo Archive; appointment book and letters: PhotoDisc, Inc.